Becoming the Teacher I Needed

Becoming the Teacher I Needed

LESSONS IN RADICAL KINDNESS AND RESILIENCE

JERE CHANG

JB JOSSEY-BASS™
A Wiley Brand

Library of Congress Cataloging-in-Publication Data is Available:

ISBN 9781394357628 (Hardback)
ISBN 9781394357642 (ePDF)
ISBN 9781394357635 (ePub)

Cover Design: Paul McCarthy
Cover Art: © Getty Images | Leocrafts
Back Cover Photograph: © Ann Packwood
SKY10154194_041526

Contents

Introduction

The Calling I Never Received

Ask most teachers why they got into this profession, and you'll likely hear something inspiring. Maybe it was a childhood love of learning, a dream of making a difference, or a calling to shape the future.

But if you were to ask me how I got into teaching, I wouldn't start with some inspirational childhood moment or a story about lining up stuffed animals for story time. I'd tell you the truth:

I simply hated school. I hated it from kindergarten through 11th grade. I'll explain later how 12th grade became a pivotal moment in my educational journey. I rarely felt seen, supported, or fully understood. I wasn't the kid who thrived in the classroom; I was the kid counting down the hours until it was over. I was the kid with a hidden disability trying to stay under the radar and constantly wondering if there was a place in the world where I might actually belong.

When it came time to choose a major in college, I did not have a clear sense of what I wanted to do, but I knew I aspired to do something that would make a difference for people like me. I wanted to break the mold. By the time graduation rolled around, I chose a career path in university administration working in residence life at my college.

And when I became a teacher, it didn't get much better. I quit my first teaching job after just one year. I made it two years at my second school, but only because my mom, also a teacher, warned me it would look really bad on my résumé to have two back-to-back one-year stints. "Just hang on a little longer," she said, so I did and it was miserable.

This is not exactly the sparkling beginning of someone writing a book about education, right? The truth is, I didn't fall in love with teaching right away. I didn't walk into the classroom and feel a surge of purpose. I walked in and felt overwhelmed, underprepared, and out of place. I spent a lot of time wondering if I had made a huge mistake; that I was not cut out for this work. In the beginning, teaching was a job where I clocked in, performed my duties, and received a paycheck, and I wanted something more.

I couldn't see it in the moment, but the messy, uncertain beginning perfectly prepared me to become the kind of teacher I needed as a child. If you'd asked me back then why I became a teacher, I probably would've mumbled something about job stability while quietly panicking over how to explain my entire résumé. There was no vision board. There was no tearful classroom epiphany. I did not have a burning desire to mold the next generation. I didn't become a teacher out of passion. I became a teacher out of … circumstance.

Master of Masking

I was 12 years old when I began to truly notice my differences. At the age when most kids are desperate to blend in, I felt as if I was on the outside looking in. I grew up in a small, conservative town and the ways I stood out weren't exactly celebrated. I was born with a condition called spina bifida, which, in my case, meant using catheters daily. On the outside, I appeared able-bodied, but every day I was managing a deeply private medical routine, quietly juggling logistics, discomfort, and the fear of being exposed. My disability wasn't visible enough to invite support, and too embarrassing to talk about openly. I became a master at masking, performing normalcy while carrying the weight of something that I did not want anyone else to see from fear of embarrassment.

I'll never forget one afternoon in seventh grade when I was late returning from the restroom as a result of managing my medical routine. When I snuck back into the classroom, my teacher stopped mid-lesson and snapped, "Where have you been? You've been gone way too long!" My face burned with embarrassment, and I wanted to crawl inside my desk. The one question I always wanted to avoid,

"What do you do in the restroom?" faced me in front of my peers. It was moments like these that taught me that school was not a safe place for people like me. People who are different and take too long in the restroom.

Years later, as a teacher, I often think about that moment. It reminds me that when a student lingers too long in the hallway, returns late from the restroom, or seems distracted, there may be a story I can't see. What may look like defiance, laziness, or carelessness could just as easily be a child quietly fighting a battle they simply don't have the words or resilience to explain. That memory keeps me gentle in my responses, slower to judge, and more intentional about creating a classroom where students don't have to fear the weight of everyone's eyes when they're already carrying more than enough.

Still, there were rare moments of light. In ninth grade, a kind English teacher pulled me aside after class and said, "You always have something interesting to say, but I don't think you realize it." It was small, but it stuck. For once, I felt noticed in a good way, and it chipped a tiny crack in the wall I'd built around myself. Just as I was beginning to find my place, something came crashing down. I was starting to discover that I was gay. The relief of finally feeling seen for my voice began colliding with the fear of being seen for who I truly was, and once again I found myself wrestling with the question of whether I could ever belong. Being gay and disabled in a place that feared difference was like living inside a locked room with no windows.

I always monitored what I said, what to share, and what version of myself felt safest that day. It was isolating, confusing, and exhausting. However, that experience and all those years of silence, shame, and survival became the foundation for everything I do as a teacher today. That complicated childhood taught me how to see those who might feel alone or invisible. It gave me the fire to advocate, to listen, to create the kind of classroom where every student feels seen not just for who they are, *but for who they're still becoming.*

Those early teaching years were rough. I didn't look like other teachers. I was quirky, silly, and did things a bit differently, but something magical happened. Slowly and quietly, I became the teacher I needed as a child. It didn't happen during a magical lesson or a perfectly executed unit plan. It happened in the weirdest, most wonderfully chaotic ways.

A kid asked if they could eat lunch in my room because "people don't talk over me here." Another said, "This is the first class where I don't feel like I have to pretend I'm not smart." One of my twice-exceptional students, gifted and navigating challenges like ADHD or anxiety, told me, "This is the only place where I feel normal," and then there was the kid who handed me a note that said, "Thank you for using the right name. I didn't think any teacher would."

That's when I knew this work was bigger than standards and lesson plans. It was about creating a space where the quirky, the brilliant, the anxious, the loud, the quiet, the queer, and the overlooked could all take a deep breath and just be. The job I once took just to "see how it goes" became the work that changed me and maybe even changed a few kids along the way.

I wasn't winning any teaching awards. My anchor charts were crooked. My inbox was a mess, but somehow, despite the chaos, these kids felt connected. They felt safe. They laughed. They learned, and they came back even when they didn't have to.

That's when it hit me. I might not have entered this profession with a calling, a Pinterest-worthy classroom, or a laminated life plan, but I have stumbled into something real. So here we are.

This book is divided into two parts.

Part I Here, I go back to a childhood spent in classrooms where I felt invisible, misunderstood, and completely out of place. This section is messy and real. It's filled with stories about what it was like to grow up disabled, queer, and completely disconnected from the place that was supposed to feel safe. There are a few classroom disasters, some awkward early teaching moments, and the kind of growth that only happens after years of figuring it out the hard way. Here I share how I went from hating school to finally getting that teacher that everyone deserves: A teacher who sees kids, honors differences, and believes in giving every child a chance.

Part II is full of research-backed strategies, reflective questions, classroom-tested wisdom, and real talk about burnout, boundaries, joy, laughter, and why some days it's okay if the biggest win is just making it to 3:30 without crying in your car. (And even if you *did* cry in your car, I still count that as resilience.)

This book is for the teachers who didn't feel called but came anyway.

It's for the ones who were told they didn't fit the mold and decided to break it.

It's for the educators who entered this profession through the side door, the back door, or by accident but stayed because something inside them clicked. However, it's also for the teachers who were called to teach and do fit the mold.

You don't have to be perfect. You don't have to love every minute, and you don't have to feel guilty if your calling didn't arrive on a cloud of glitter and laminated lesson plans.

Teaching isn't always pretty, but it's powerful, and sometimes, the best teachers are the ones who never saw it coming, so grab your coffee, your flair pens, and whatever leftover snack a kindergartener handed you at dismissal. Welcome. You belong here.

PART I

The Stories That Shaped Me

Introduction

Section one begins long before I decorated my first classroom, attended my first professional development session, wrote rigorous lesson plans, and before my first disappointing teacher evaluation. It begins in the formative years when school felt like a place where I simply had to survive and did not belong. This section is about the version of me who wanted to fit in but discovered that I was better often hiding in plain sight.

These chapters aren't polished, but they're the moments that shaped me before I even imagined becoming a teacher. They explore what it feels like to grow up queer and disabled in a small conservative town. This portion of the book dives into the awkward, painful, and sometimes humorous path of a kid who didn't love school but somehow managed to grow up into an adult who transformed it for others.

Honestly, you may find this part a bit messy, because that's exactly what those years were for me. Here you'll discover why I teach the way that I do, why I respond with grace when a child takes too long in the restroom, and why I strive to advocate for all children especially the children who feel like outsiders. These are the roots that taught me that children need adults who see them fully, even the parts they're trying to hide.

Part I is where I lay down the truth of what shaped me, not only as an educator, but as a compassionate human. It's where I explore how a child who hated school became an adult determined to build classrooms where students feel seen, heard, safe, and celebrated regardless of their background.

So, let's begin there, before the calling, before the confidence, and the teacher I eventually became. Let's start with the kid who never imagined she would write a book about becoming the teacher I needed as a child.

CHAPTER 1

Designing My Journey

"I quit!" Those were the last words I spoke to my principal. Tears streamed down my face as I made my way to my car. On the drive home, a mixed flood of relief, doubt, and frustration consumed me. This was the second school I had walked away from in just three years. Would I ever find a school that would appreciate my quirky, fun-loving teaching style? Was it too late to change paths? Would I ever find a job that granted me the basic freedom to use the restroom when I needed, pay my bills without anxiety, and earn the respect that I had been seeking? Why had I chosen a career that so often feels thankless, draining, and disrespected? Well as I mentioned earlier, I didn't choose teaching, teaching chose me. Let me take you back in time to the 1900s—a time before smartphones, social media, and, for me, direction.

I graduated from North Georgia College in 1995 with a B.S. in Outdoor Leisure Recreation and Leisure Studies. If you're wondering what that even means, trust me you're not alone. I can practically hear the jokes now. A degree in playing outside? Not exactly. I loved the outdoors and dreamed of working as a park ranger in one of the national parks like the Grand Canyon, Bryce Canyon, or even Yellowstone. The idea of spending my days among red rocks, canyons, and endless skies felt like the perfect life. But as my final year of college ticked by, reality knocked. One afternoon, the Residence

Life Coordinator called me into her office. She closed the door, smiled knowingly, and said, "I think you should apply for my job." She was planning to resign at the end of the year. I'd been a Resident Assistant (RA) for two years, managing dorm life, solving problems, and occasionally corralling wayward freshmen. Apparently, she thought I had a gift for working with people. I was months away from graduating with zero direction and no clue what came next. But this? This job came with a salary, an apartment, and utilities. It was everything I needed to avoid moving back to my hometown.

So, I said yes.

By my second year as the Residence Life Coordinator, I was coasting through the motions of my first professional job, and I did not have much thought about my future. So, when the Dean called me in for a meeting, I wasn't exactly prepared for a deep dive into my life plans.

"What's next for you?" she asked seemingly expecting some well thought out plan. However, I replied, "Next, what do you mean, next? I'm comfortable here."

She laughed, "You're doing great here, but there's not much room to climb. If you really want to advance in this field, you'll need to pursue a degree in College Student Affairs Administration," and just like that, I found myself packing for the University of Georgia.

I enrolled in a two-year master's program and took an assistantship in the Department of Academic Enhancement. It was steady, predictable work that looked good on paper. By my final year, the Director of Academic Enhancement pulled me aside and offered me a full-time position as Coordinator for Academic Enhancement in Residence Life. It wasn't glamorous, but I jumped at the chance, because it felt like the first real step toward something bigger in college student affairs. Who knows? Maybe one day, I'd even land a role as a dean... or higher.

The job was a full-time respectable position at the University of Georgia and it sounded like the kind of work that should've left me feeling fulfilled. I spent my days guiding freshmen students into a newly discovered world of university life. I facilitated academic workshops and counseled students in study techniques, time management, reading strategies, and communication. I hired and managed teams of peer tutors. It was a decent job, but I could barely afford to pay my rent, and boredom crept in like fog. I was broke, listless, and worn thin by the quiet misery that comes with realizing you're stuck somewhere you no longer belong. It was in that haze of frustration that I finally made a choice, and for the first time, I carved out a path for myself, by myself.

Working at a large university had its perks, and I wasn't about to let them go to waste. With the campus at my fingertips, I dove headfirst into another master's degree program fully funded by the university. I chose to study Teaching English to Speakers of Other Languages, with an emphasis on Applied Linguistics. Back then, my sights were set far beyond the familiar streets of Athens, Georgia. I pictured myself teaching English in the quiet corners of Japan, the bustling cities of South Korea, or maybe beneath the sunlit skies of Spain. But life, as it often does, had other ideas. In two swift years, I earned the degree, but somewhere along the way, something shifted. I fell in love, and just like that, the dream of distant shores began to blur, replaced by something softer, something that whispered of staying right where I was, so I began exploring options near home.

For the first time in my life, I felt a real career passion. The kind that keeps you awake at night, flipping through books just for the thrill of it. I'd fallen hard for sociolinguistics, this fascinating web where language and society tangled together, shaping one another in ways I'd never noticed before. It was more than just words and grammar. It was identity, power, belonging, and the subtle shifts in speech that could tell a whole story about who someone was and the world they moved through. So yet again, I decided to change careers. Unfortunately, the job market for people with degrees in TESOL was, unsurprisingly, limited to teaching, so I pursued a teaching job teaching high school ESOL.

When I told my current Director about my plans, she laughed. Shock and disappointment crushed me. When I asked her to elaborate, she began to describe the state of public teaching. She said I was embarking upon a thankless career and one in which I would find little to no success. As anger began to overtake, I explained that I was accustomed to working in a thankless position as I would be earning $20,000 more per year working fewer days per year. Again, she laughed and explained that I was naïve to believe that money was the core of success. Although I agree with her sentiment, I was angered at the notion of someone making a six-figure salary telling someone making $28,000 a year that money is simply not important. I sat there, soaking in the words of someone I admired professionally, and began to believe that I had just made one of the biggest mistakes of my life.

One Step Closer to Thriving

I never set out to become an ESOL teacher, but like many educators, my career took a path I had not entirely planned. I immediately found myself drawn to working with multilingual learners. Helping students navigate not only high school but also an entirely new language and culture became my passion. I felt challenged, inspired, and committed to language acquisition and student advocacy.

However, as many teachers will tell you, passion doesn't pay the bills. Needing additional income, I took on a summer side job teaching an adult-level linguistics course for educators working toward their ESOL endorsement. It was a perfect fit. My expertise in language acquisition, combined with my real-world classroom experience, made me an effective instructor for teachers who wanted to better serve English language learners. I taught them the theories, methodologies, and strategies they would soon implement in their own classrooms. In essence, I was preparing them to do the very work I was already doing in public schools.

Despite my qualifications and experience, the Georgia Professional Standards Commission later informed me that I did not meet the requirements to teach in public schools. The irony was hard to ignore. I was considered qualified enough to train educators in linguistics, second language acquisition, and instructional best practices, but I was deemed unqualified to teach public school students. It was one of those moments when bureaucracy overshadowed logic, and I could not help but question the system. If I was good enough to prepare teachers, why was I not qualified to teach the very students they would soon be working with?

There I was, qualified to teach adults but not teenagers, leaving me to navigate public education on a provisional certificate. Apparently, the universe has a sense of humor, because, yet again, I found myself enrolling in another M.Ed. program with a focus on teaching ESOL for K-12. I did not realize it at the time, but my teaching journey was just beginning, because one thing rang true in that high school classroom. I had a knack for teaching.

When I stood in front of my classroom with my quirky sense of humor, I captivated my high school students. In my classroom, I was a big fish in a small pond, but in the overall scope of the school, I was invisible. From my point of view, I was seen as "just a teacher" trying to help English language learners meet data goals. My first year of teaching in public school was a division of two worlds. In one world, I found myself inspiring and impacting high school students giving them language skills to help them and their families survive in a country where they were hoping to achieve their dreams. In the other world, I was immersed in curriculum and data analysis meetings. Sadly, the data always seemed to win. My principal often inquired about benchmark assessments and asked me to set data goals for my students. I would share stories about how José got a job and now helps support his family, or how Emilia helps her mom understand the doctor's recent diagnosis and treatment plan for her younger brother to which my administration would reply, "But are your students on track to meet their end of year testing goals?" I was beginning to believe that my former director was right, but knowing that I was making a difference, I refused to let the reality of the push of standardized testing in public-schools squash my dreams.

By the time second semester rolled around, my principal was in full Oprah mode. Contracts for the next school year were seemingly given to any interested teacher willing to return. "You get a contract! You get a contract! Everybody gets a contract!" Well, almost everybody. Somehow, I was the only one left standing without a job for the upcoming school year. At first, I thought maybe mine had just slipped between the cracks of her desk or gotten lost in the latest installment of a copy machine jam, and after weeks of stressing out about my future employment, I decided to ask.

"Oh, don't worry," she said with a kind of nonchalance reserved for people who have jobs lined up for the upcoming school year. "You'll get your contract."

Summer crept closer, and my inbox remained suspiciously empty. When the final bell rang and the students poured out of the building ready for summer vacation, I still didn't have a contract.

"Relax," she repeated, waving me off. "You'll get it over the summer."

What she didn't know was that during the first week of summer break, my phone rang with a new possibility. The voice on the other end wasn't offering vague reassurance, they were inviting me to apply to a newly opened school near my home.

What? You've got to be joking! Kindergarten? First grade? No way! There is no way I am teaching little kids. "My voice echoed through the phone with both disbelief and sheer terror. My former TESOL professor, the one who'd once told me I was bound for greatness, suggested I trade in teenage angst for the sticky fingers and boundless energy of elementary schoolers. She said all the right things to convince me to make the leap into early elementary school." What did she say exactly? In full transparency, I can't recall, but I remember her saying all the right things I needed to make the leap to kindergarten.

It was something along the lines of, "You're dynamic," "You're such an inspiration," and "I just know you'll be exactly what these little kids need."

Knowing I hadn't signed a contract with my current high school, I reached out to the administrators of the elementary school and scheduled an interview. The interview seemed to be a formality as my former professor had highly recommended me; however, I shared my classroom management plan, knowledge of primary education, and even asked a few questions in return. I emerged victorious and accepted a job as a kindergarten and first-grade English Language Arts teacher at a K-1 elementary school. All I had to do was send an email resigning from my current high school position.

However, I never considered the possibility of my former principal denying my resignation. She replied explaining that she was not going to let me out of my contract, and if I failed to comply, I would lose my teacher certification. As a wry smile smirked across my lips, I sent one of my all-time favorite career emails.

Dear Principal ______,

    I appreciate having the opportunity to work for you at ________ School. I understand your need to hold your employees to their signed contracts. However, I am not one of those employees. If you check your records closely, you'll see that I have not received a contract for the upcoming school year. I wish you the best of luck in the upcoming school year.

Sincerely,
A Teacher One Step Closer to Thriving

Let's just say I burned that bridge. She replied accusing me of being unprofessional and saying a few other things along the lines of me not caring about my students. Seemingly, she was trying to tap into teacher guilt by suggesting that I do not care about students, and it worked a little. As the guilt began to settle in, I felt as if I was abandoning my students, but then it hit me! Students are everywhere. I am not "abandoning" former students, I am gearing up to inspire future students.

I leaned back in my chair, a smug smile gracing my lips. *"Jere, don't let other people design your journey!"* I mimicked my grandma's voice, her words echoing through my memory and paving the way toward a more confident and resilient self.

Fear of Small Humans

I'll never forget the week before my first day as a kindergarten teacher. I was afraid. I am not sure what I was afraid of: little kids, helicopter parents, change, but I was terrified. Many people view me as a thriving and confident elementary teacher, but to this day, I begin every single school year afraid of failure, scared of the unknown, and still often ask myself, "How did I get here?"

There's a song, *Once in a Lifetime*, by Talking Heads[1] that summed up my feelings perfectly:

And you may find yourself living in a shotgun shack
And you may find yourself in another part of the world
And you may find yourself behind the wheel of a large automobile
And you may find yourself in a beautiful house, with a beautiful wife
And you may ask yourself, "Well, how did I get here?"

Why had I not achieved the dreams that I correlated with success, respect, and financial freedom? Here I was, a supposed adult, living in a shoebox of an apartment, an hour away from the place I'd sworn to leave behind. My trusty Honda Civic, a relic from my college days, was my sanctuary, a place where my unknown dreams would eventually come true, a place of solitude, or so I'd thought. I felt utterly adrift, so I did what any sensible adult would do, I drove home and called my mom.

My mom was a middle school teacher. I'll get to her a bit later; however, becoming a teacher was a dream she thought she would never achieve as someone who didn't go to college until later in life. A former factory worker and single mother of four, she was a proud teacher, and when I called saying that I was disappointed in myself for aspiring to be "just a teacher," she shut me down immediately. I had surrounded myself with friends who had careers that were deemed as "more successful": doctors, corporate, attorneys, professors, etc.

My mom shared stories about how former students reached out to her explaining how she impacted their lives in ways that she had never imagined possible. One of her former students had recently been accepted into Harvard. She saw another young adult working at the local supermarket, and while scanning my mom's groceries, my mom's former student shared her love of reading as a direct result of my mom's guidance. One by one, my mom shared stories of the

---

[1] Talking Heads. *Once in a Lifetime*. Lyrics by David Byrne, Brian Eno, Chris Frantz, Jerry Harrison, and Tina Weymouth. © Wb Music Corp., MCA Music Ltd., E.G. Music Ltd., Index Music Inc., Universal/MCA Music Ltd., Universal Music MGB Ltd., Status One Music, and Index Music, Inc.

impact she had made in her students' lives. My mom beamed with pride, and I slowly began to believe that one day, maybe I too could make an impact in the lives of my students.

I felt a bit better about my career aspirations; however, one thing my mom couldn't assuage was my fear of little kids. I'm not saying I had pedophobia, yes, a fear of small children is a real thing, but their unpredictable nature frightened me. Although adults can also be unpredictable, it's kids that remind me of squirrels who dart out in front of cars in such a way that results in the driver slamming on the brakes, thus causing all the passengers to lunge forward, spilling their drinks, losing their fries, and questioning their spiritual beliefs. Fortunately for me my sister was a first-grade teacher at that time, so I reached out to her for some expert advice.

I called her and expressed that there was one big fear looming over me.

She said, "Let me guess… parents?"

"Absolutely not! Adults are easy. I can reason with adults."

She laughed and said, "You say that now, but just wait and see," and honestly, she was right. I didn't fully get it until I started teaching, but it turns out, reasoning with adults, yeah, that's not really a thing.

I said, "No, my biggest fear is getting the class to go places. How do I get the entire class from point A to B?"

Laughing, she replied, "What are you talking about?"

"How do I get all the kids to go to lunch, recess, art? How do I transport them from place to place?" Yes, I literally used the word "transport" as if I were working logistics for a delivery service. She gave me a few tips about creating a specific line order by assigning a number to each kid, lining up by tables where the kids sit, etc., but my fears loomed.

She gave other helpful advice like waiting to create student labels until after the first day of school. "Labels? Why do I need student labels? They can't read!"

"Exactly! That's the point," she replied.

"Why would anyone think I was a good fit to teach young children?" I thought to myself as I hung up the phone.

Then came the big day. Twenty-three tiny humans, a kaleidoscope of bright eyes and nervous smiles filled my classroom. It took all my willpower to corral them into their assigned seats, and a wave of relief washed over me when I finally achieved some illusion of order. Unfortunately, my triumph was short-lived. It did not take me long to realize I should have listened to my sister when it came to waiting to make student labels. You see, I'd foolishly ignored my sister's advice and labeled everything before I met my students, their families, and/or caregivers. I threw caution to the wind, and I labeled everything: cubbies, desks, agendas, folders: EVERYTHING!

Apparently, many children go by nicknames, middle names, abbreviated names, etc. Who knew that school records are often riddled with a minefield of misspellings and mistakes? Who knows? Experienced teachers, that's who knows. My students, despite their non-reading abilities, pointed out my errors, and I felt a blush creep up my neck. As someone with a simple yet complicated first name J-e-r-e, I am careful to spell and pronounce names correctly. Like a whirlwind, I set off to make the corrections around the room: cubbies, folders, the bulletin board, desk labels, etc., and in that moment, I accepted the fate that although I am intelligent and competent, accepting advice and guidance from experienced teachers, can, at times, prove beneficial. "Hey younger teacher self! Asking for help is not a sign of weakness. It's a crucial step towards becoming a more successful teacher."

I decided to postpone my label catastrophe and summoned the troops. My little army of kindergartners wriggled and giggled on the brightly colored carpet; their assigned squares were each decorated with letters, shapes, and animals. They eyed me with a mixture of curiosity and suspicion, seemingly asking, "Who is this strange lady secretly afraid of children?" And just like that the first of many "Morning Meetings" took place. I took a deep breath and launched into my greeting, and then something magical happened. I was funny! I made them laugh! I really made them laugh! The tension melted away and was replaced by a wave of giggles and curiosity. I created a safe space, a place where mistakes were not only tolerated but encouraged. My classroom was a place to stumble, fall, blossom, and grow. Somewhere along the way, I even managed to teach them a few things! The kids adored me. Parents showered me with praise. It was glorious, but somewhere between the hugs and the high fives, I realized that popularity wasn't the same as success.

Record Scratch

I will never forget my first official observation as a kindergarten teacher. My principal came in with her clipboard in hand and sat in the back of the room like a hawk eyeing its prey. I started my lesson, which entailed reading a story about a mischievous monkey. While reading, I facilitated a classroom discussion about making predictions. I watched with pride as my students, a whirlwind of energy and curiosity, eagerly participated. They answered questions, asked insightful questions of their own, and their eyes sparkled with excitement. My principal hung around for about 10 minutes, smiled, and as she walked out of my classroom she said, "I'll email you to schedule a conference to discuss and sign off on your observation." A sense of accomplishment washed over me. I had found my calling! I was making a difference, nurturing young minds, and I was engaged.

Later that week, I strutted into her office, chest puffed out, ready to bask in the glow of her praise. Instead, the wind was knocked out of me. "Where was your learning objective?" she asked, her tone surprisingly stern. Next, and I wish I was fabricating this story, she demonstrated the proper way for me to sneeze. Apparently, I had sneezed into my hand as opposed to my inner elbow where my arm bends. Yes, reader, I do know the most hygienic way to sneeze, and I understand that sneezing into one's hands may lead to spreading germs, but of all the things to discuss in my first formal observation, I honestly believe that sneezing habits should fall low on the list. Surely, there were more important things to address, but then came the gavel.

"Your students seem a bit, hmm, unruly," she said, her voice dripping with disapproval.

I sat there, stunned. Where were the compliments? The words of encouragement? Of course, it's her job as my administrator to guide me to be a better and more effective teacher; I understand this, but surely, I was doing something right. From my point of view, I saw a classroom filled with engaged students, waving their hands in the air, ready to join in the discussion and share their thirst for learning. I saw a kindergarten community, a family, a space where students were allowed to explore and learn all while being themselves: kids.

I launched into a defensive tirade, listing all my accomplishments. She listened patiently, acknowledging my efforts, but her final words cut through my indignation: "It's my job to help you grow as a teacher, and as a first-year teacher, you have so much to learn." I left her office feeling deflated, my initial enthusiasm was replaced by a wave of dejection.

Once home, I threw my bag onto the floor, dropped onto the couch, and called my mom. Tears streamed down my face as I poured out my frustrations, my exhaustion, and my sense of failure. "I can't do this anymore, Mom," I sobbed. "I'm done. I'm quitting." On the other end of the line, my mother's voice was steady and calm. "You can't quit," she reassured me. "Your students deserve you, and just like her mother used to tell her she said, *Jere, don't let other people design your journey.*"

Torn between the desire to flee from it all and the nagging guilt that came with abandoning my students once again, my mom had a point. My students deserved the teacher I needed as a child, and I deserved to enjoy a career that I had chosen. Teachers deserve to love teaching without feeling the pressures of only doing it "for the kids." Still feeling a bit down, I agreed to finish the year and give my students the best version of me, because regardless of my principal's onslaught of critiques, I had something to offer my students.

Weeks later, as the school year dragged on and my stress deepened, my mom called, sensing my growing frustration. I confided in her that I was determined to leave at the end of the school year. I could not handle the constant feeling of failure. I wanted to pursue a career where I could feel just a glimmer of hope and success. She paused for a moment, then offered a piece of advice that changed everything. "I know you're struggling but hear me out. Stay for two years."

I snapped. "What? Another year? No way! I can't possibly consider spending another year in such a toxic environment."

"It's not just about finishing the year," she explained. "If you leave after one year, it will look bad on your resume. Trust me. When you're looking for new positions, future schools will see that you've only been at your first two schools for a year each. They'll see it as a red flag as if you can't stick it out. Two years shows you've committed. It will give you credibility."

Reluctantly, I agreed. I would stay. I would stay a second year, give it my best shot, and after that, I would reassess.

I vividly remember the first day of my second year at that school. I was determined to make it better, to make myself better, but despite my best efforts, despite all the new strategies and self-talk, I couldn't shake the feeling that I was still failing.

At my previous university job, though I found myself growing increasingly bored with the routine, I always had a voice. My opinions and knowledge were often well received even though I was neither a manager nor a director. I wasn't just another cog in the wheel. I was seen; I was heard. I had the autonomy to make suggestions, to offer new ideas, to navigate decisions alongside those in superior positions. That freedom, that sense of ownership, had fueled my passion, and I carried that same determination with me when I stepped into the classroom for the first time as a public-school teacher.

What I didn't know then was that in the world of public K-12 education, especially in a place as rigid and bureaucratic as this one, the concept of "being seen" was a luxury. I was "just another teacher," expected to follow a literal call and response lesson script. My ideas, no matter how well-intentioned, no matter how relevant to the needs of my students, were mostly met with indifference, or even worse, dismissiveness.

I remember one grade-level meeting where all the kindergarten teachers and administrators sat around a table to discuss how we could best support our English Language Learners. The administrators were leading the conversation, and it quickly became clear they were determined to implement the "I say, you say, we say" method as the core approach to teaching. While there may be some value to this method such as practice and reinforcing pronunciation, I couldn't help but feel like it was a one-size-fits-all solution to a much more complex issue.

I knew my students weren't just going to magically learn a language through repetitive drills. They needed more than that. They needed emotional and social context, connection, something real to hold on to. With all the enthusiasm I could muster, I brought up my passion for social–emotional learning (SEL). In full transparency, at the time, I had never heard of SEL learning, so I simply suggested integrating more informal and casual conversations into the classroom to help my students navigate language in real-world scenarios, to build their confidence and overall conversational skills.

To me, SEL is essential. Although I could not quite articulate it or back my ideas up with research at that time, I strongly believe that students who feel safe and comfortable in school are more likely to achieve academic success. I was learning and growing as a newly minted teacher, but I knew that I wanted my classroom to be more than a place of drills and repetition. It needed to be a space where students could express themselves, be heard, and start to trust their voices. Unfortunately, in that meeting, instead of my ideas being met with curiosity or discussion, I felt the sharp sting of dismissal. The administrators were dead set on the I-say-you-say-we-say method. There was no room for my "fluffy" ideas.

In hindsight, I can see how I came across: like a child protesting their homework, saying it was boring without understanding the "why" behind the structure. I lacked the tools, the research, and the professional language to back up my point of view. I didn't understand then that SEL wasn't just a trend, it was a proven approach that could improve academic performance, foster a positive classroom environment, and, ultimately, lead to greater success for my students.[2] If I had taken the time to properly research and present my ideas, maybe they would have listened, but then again, I have my doubts.

Throughout the second year I did what I was told. I followed the prescribed methods, taught the standards, and focused on the data. I performed in such a way that earns checkmarks on the state-mandated rubric. The checklist that administrators carry around to monitor compliance guided my intentions. The rubric wasn't concerned with whether my students were engaged or whether they were learning in the true sense of the word. It only measured whether I was following the protocol set forth by people who hadn't set foot in a classroom in years, if ever.

---

[2] Yale School of Medicine. "Research Finds Social and Emotional Learning Produces Significant Benefits for Students: Academic Performance, Well-Being, and Perceptions of School Safety All Improved." Yale School of Medicine, July 14, 2023. Accessed October 2025. https://medicine.yale.edu/news-article/new-research-published-in-child-development-confirms-social-and-emotional-learning-significantly-improves-student-academic-performance-well-being-and-perceptions-of-school-safety/.

I fell into the routine of it. I stopped questioning the methods that didn't work. I began to perform, just like they expected me to, all the while feeling like a small part of a much larger system that didn't have the space or desire to hear the voices of its teachers or students. During this second year, I continued to long for a place, a school, a career, anywhere that would nurture not just the academic side of a child, but their whole self. I longed for a utopia where the love of learning wasn't confined to the pursuit of data points or standardized tests but was allowed to flourish in its many forms. Surely, there was a school or institution that existed that valued students as more than just numbers, that ignited curiosity, creativity, and the unique rhythm of each learner.

I Like Your Shoes

Living in a large city like Atlanta gave me access to an array of options: private schools, Montessori, charter schools, and public institutions to name a few, but despite the variety, nothing seemed to fully align with my vision. Then, one day, during my many online searches I stumbled upon a charter school in Atlanta. Its mission was clear: to provide students from underfunded areas with an equitable shot at success, offering a sanctuary where their potential could be nurtured beyond the confines of traditional educational limitations. On the surface, it seemed like the perfect place where both teaching and learning could be approached with love and empathy. I applied, full of hope, but weeks passed without so much as a phone call. It was then that I realized the cold truth: this school was a dream for many educators, not just me. Its reputation had made it a sought-after employment opportunity in the city, and the competition was fierce.

For a while, I entertained the thought that perhaps I was destined to work in a school that was determined to check boxes and stifle the creativity of teachers like me. I began exploring other options, even contemplating a path toward higher education academia. I thought about applying to PhD programs with the hope that one day I might find fulfillment in a university setting yet again, but after obtaining three master's degrees, the thought of reenrolling into yet another graduate level program was not something I wanted to take on.

Just when I thought I had resigned myself to this path, something unexpected happened. I attended a dinner party hosted by an old friend. This random dinner party turned out to be a pivotal moment in my life. Like most dinner parties, the room buzzed with the kind of superficial chatter that fills the spaces between moments. Strangers stood in clusters, smiling politely, exchanging pleasantries with others with whom they would likely never meet again. I was, as usual, an outsider in my own skin. I stood alone in a crowded kitchen balancing a drink in one hand and a paper plate piled with an assortment of bite-sized snacks from the charcuterie board in the other.

Despite my online presence, which often leads people to assume I am the life of the party, the truth is quite the opposite. I am awkwardly shy in new and/or unfamiliar environments. When surrounded by unfamiliar faces, I often find myself standing off to the side, observing, imagining stories for the people around me, crafting elaborate tales about who they are, what secrets they carry, and how their lives might unfold. Until I can find someone with whom I can connect, I typically stand around like a lost schoolgirl looking for a lunch table filled with people with whom I can relate.

As I was busy weaving my latest narrative about a group of four people gathered at a nearby table, a woman approached me. She was confident in a way that I wasn't, but I tried to muster a smile as she struck up a conversation. I nervously stabbed a cube of cheese with a toothpick and popped it into my mouth, only to realize too late that she had paused, waiting for me to respond. I was completely lost in the conversation, my mind already on something else, as it often is. Flustered, I blurted out the first thing that came to mind. "I like your shoes," I said, pointing awkwardly at her feet.

For anyone who has ever lived in a mind full of distractions, you learn a few tricks to stay afloat in social situations. One of those tricks is to offer a compliment when you've missed the thread of conversation. Just say something simple and universally agreeable. It's a way of pretending that you're engaged when, in fact, the distractions surrounding you are craving your attention.

The woman's face lit up. "Oh, thank you! These are the perfect shoes for teaching," she said, glancing down at her footwear.

Teaching? My ears perked up, my attention snapping back to the moment. A connection. This is something I can talk about.

"Are you a teacher?" I asked, eager to keep the conversation going.

She nodded and explained that she was a consultant for a local charter school. As we dug deeper into our exchange, I realized that she was a partner at the very school I had applied to months earlier but had never received a response.

"No way! I applied to that school," I said, my voice a mix of surprise and hope," but I never heard back from them."

She paused, considering my words, then smiled, "Give me a couple of days. I'll reach out to the principal directly and put in a good word for you."

I didn't quite believe her, but I nodded along, too stunned to do anything else. I hoped that she would remember our short conservation and reach out to the school thus affording me an opportunity for an interview. I felt confident that I could get the job if I could just get an in-person interview. The challenge wasn't proving I was the right fit, it was getting past the automated application systems, the checklist-style qualifications, and the impersonal screenings that couldn't capture what I brought to the table. Once I landed an interview, that was my moment. I could tell my story, share my vision, and make them see beyond the bullet points on my résumé. It wasn't about being the most qualified on paper, it was about showing them, face-to-face, that I was the teacher their students needed.

A week later, I received the call. The principal of the charter school wanted to schedule an in-person interview that involved me teaching a lesson to a current kindergarten class. That phone call led to the opportunity of earning a teaching position at the very school I researched and sought out. As predicted, I nailed the interview and lesson, and without hesitation, I eagerly accepted a first-grade teaching position for the upcoming school year.

I humbly share this story with you, dear reader, not as a tale of serendipity, but as a reminder: you never know who you're talking to. Every conversation, even the most mundane or awkward, has the potential to lead to something life changing. So, be kind. Be confident. And when in doubt, shoot your shot.

CHAPTER 2

The World's OK-est Teacher

Eager to start my new school, I decided to invest my whole self into this new school and community, so much in fact that I bought my first home near the school. I found a 700 sq ft condo near the school. My life was modest and simple, but it was mine, and I was on top of the world. My dreams of moving to a bustling city overseas never happened, but I was excited to start a new life in Atlanta.

I always tell teachers that starting a new school poses many challenges regardless of one's experience. You must learn new ways of doing things like making copies, requesting time off, submitting maintenance requests, building your reputation, proving your worth, and who has the keys to the office supply closet. Spoiler alert: it's usually one of the front desk staff folks. For me it goes without saying, but I highly recommend building relationships with the folks with keys and access to food: cafeteria staff, custodial staff, front desk staff, maintenance staff, because although these are neither our managers nor sign our paychecks, it's the people with the keys and access to food who can make or break a teacher's day to day happiness.

It did not take me long to settle into my new school, and before long I developed a reputation as the fun teacher with high expectations. I add the "high expectations" part, because "fun teachers" are often assumed to not value growth and achievement among their students, but I can assure you that there are many ways to teach effectively. Students can achieve academic success in "fun" classrooms.

I was the teacher who danced the Tootsee Roll with her class after every Friday after a week of learning. If you're asking, "What's the Tootsee Roll?" I am going to assume you were not born in the 1900s. The Tootsee Roll was a popular hip-hop dance that originated in the mid-1990s, inspired by the song "Tootsee Roll" by 69 Boyz. © The song became a hit in clubs and at parties, known for its catchy beat and simple dance moves. Regardless of the students' weekly performance, I invited all interested students to the front of the classroom to celebrate the end of the school week. "The butterfly? Uh-uh, that's old. Let me see the Tootsee Roll...." To this very day, when I run into former students, young adults making lives for themselves, they often say, "I remember our class dancing the Tootsee Roll every Friday." Before introverted readers chastise me by saying, "I'd hate that," no worries, dancing was always optional, and uninterested kids were invited to opt out, watch, tap to the beat, read, color, etc.

I was the teacher who took the time to get to know my students, have fun with my students, get to know their families, and create a fun and safe space for all my students regardless of ability or background. I believe in my students regardless of their dream or ability. I became the teacher that I needed as a child. I found my school, my community, and yes, my calling.

My confidence and happiness began to grow as I was one of the most sought-after teachers at my school. Parents would share their excitement when they discovered their child was assigned to my class. My students were thriving and so was I until I was not. One year my school had a few administrative changes, which can pose a challenge for established teachers. When new leaders take over, all teachers must start over and prove their effectiveness, regardless of their former reputation and experience.

Proficiently Three

During my fourth year at my new school, a school where I was thriving, my new assistant principal scheduled a formal observation. Knowing I must once again prove my effectiveness, I made sure to plan an engaging lesson and do "all the right things" and check all the "right boxes." At the same time, I wanted to stay true to my authentic self and continue to be the fun, loving, and quirky teacher where kids feel safe to learn, grow, and make mistakes.

Maybe I'm too confident in myself, because just like my former school, I felt as if I nailed the observation. My assistant principal scheduled a follow-up meeting to discuss the observation. But unlike my former school principal who focused on my sneezing etiquette, my assistant principal began the meeting with compliments, "Your scholars are engaged. You have created such a positive classroom environment. I want other teachers to observe your teaching style. Your content is rigorous." Personally, I am not a fan of buzzwords like "scholar" and "rigorous," to describe an elementary classroom; however, I beamed with delight as she continued to sing my praises. "You're doing everything right, Ms. Chang! And with that your official teacher observation rating is a three out of four." She explained that I am a "proficient" teacher and would earn a three rating on a four-point scale. Feeling disheartened and angry, I pushed back.

Wait! Hold up! How can you say I'm doing everything right yet declare me "proficient" as opposed to "exemplary?" She went on to explain that I failed to understand the state department's teacher observation rubric. She said to be considered an "exemplary" teacher, I must be doing all the right things as well as serving as a "teacher leader." I argued that a teacher observation should reflect how I teach. Do I inspire my students? Are my lessons engaging and "rigorous?" Again, she explained that I was falling short in serving as a leader at my school, and she ended the meeting suggesting I hang more anchor charts in my classroom.

I left the meeting feeling completely dejected, but more importantly like I had something to prove. I knew I was a dynamic teacher beloved by many, including my administration. I was bound and determined not to let a rubric designed by folks far removed from the classroom design my journey. I felt confident that I was the teacher who impacted the lives of my students and gave them a love of school and learning, an experience that I never had as a child. Looking back, I wish I had solely focused on my passion for teaching, but instead, I became obsessed with being a four out of four.

I'm sure that administrators feel that it's their job to help teachers continue to develop and grow, as it's a teacher's position to help their students grow and develop regardless of ability and achievement. However, I wish more administrators had the confidence and flexibility to score their teachers in such a way that inspired teachers without making teachers feel deflated. Maybe this concept just inspired my next book idea.

Checkmate

In my evaluation, I failed to upload evidence and documents for things I was doing beyond the classroom. In my quest to become a four-star teacher, I decided to create something new for our school, and, in my opinion, it only seemed fitting for the gifted teacher to create a Chess Club. I created a Google interest form and asked our principal to post the interest form in the school newsletter. I hoped approximately 5–10 chess kids would sign up for my little club. Little did I know that my Chess Club would become the hottest club in all of Atlanta. My simple Google interest form yielded over one hundred responses; therefore, I created two clubs: grades K-2 and 3–5. I met with the school social worker to determine the most equitable way to accept participants. I spent hours creating lessons, communicating with families, and starting our school's first ever chess club. I stayed after school two days every week to lead my two clubs. I found and entered my students in local tournaments. Yes! This meant spending many Saturdays or weeknights competing in chess tournaments. And since I'm sharing my quest to be "exemplary," I feel a need to add that I led this club without a stipend or bonus. However, I absolutely loved giving kids the gift of chess. Kids who have never heard of chess were winning trophies that would be proudly displayed in our school's trophy case at the front of the school. Certainly, this would earn me my coveted extra star.

Midway through the year my assistant principal scheduled my teacher observation, and again I nailed it. I facilitated an engaging rigorous lesson in a positive classroom environment. The kids were enthusiastic and engaged in the lesson. The lesson was "rigorous" and "standards based" as expected. The following week I walked into the assistant principal's office anticipating my 4-star rating. She proceeded to shed light on my teaching effectiveness and praised the award-winning Chess Club, and just like that she shared my overall rating. Once again, I earned a three "proficient" out of four possible points "exemplary."

I recounted the evidence and documentation of all the things I did that went above and beyond my classroom expectations. Surely, I was "exemplary." Surprisingly, she agreed and said she'd reach out to the principal and reschedule a meeting with me. The following week she stopped by my classroom and explained that my efforts have "been noted." However, because my areas of "four" were limited to a few areas and not widely spread out, my overall rating would remain a three. There I stood a mere three. The teacher whom kids adored, the teacher who spent countless hours outside contracted time creating opportunities for students, the teacher who uploaded the evidence proving my merit was seen as a three in the eyes of my administrators, and this simply made me sad. I'm embarrassed to admit that I cried.

All my efforts, hard work, love of teaching, impacting students all summed up with a few checks on a rubric that deemed me as average. I spent a few weeks feeling sorry for myself, researching adjacent careers, and contemplating a career where I could thrive, but something inside me still burned. My students deserved me. They deserved a teacher who truly loves teaching. A teacher who wants to make a difference. They deserved a four out of four teacher. From that moment forward I decided to forget about observational ratings and to be the teacher that I needed as a child, but my sadness loomed.

At the end of the year, I decided a change would give me the career boost I needed, so I approached my principal and asked her to "loop up" (moving to the next grade level while keeping all the same students) to second grade. She proceeded to tell me I'm too dynamic and she needed me to stay in 1st grade, because I was the teacher that parents often requested. The teacher who kids loved.

Learning to advocate for myself I asked, "Am I being held back from achieving my career aspirations because I am 'too good'?" After a few meetings and continual persistence, my principal agreed to let me move up to second grade.

CHAPTER 3

When "Average" Teachers Thrive

I continued to feel a bit dejected about being labeled a three out of four. However, I was excited about the opportunity to work with the same students for a second year. I had one of those "good" classes. I am not using "good" to describe behavior or achievement, I use the word "good" to describe the perfect fit between a teacher and her students.

Out of twenty-five students, ten identified as "gifted," and several others were high achievers, the kind of kids who soared past expectations. I was able to facilitate an experience centered around creative and divergent thinking. It was a vibe, and we were thriving despite the presence of the state's rigid teacher evaluation rubric. The state created teacher observation rubric demanded I differentiate for my students while refusing to extend the same courtesy to me. In our classroom, boxes and rubrics were replaced with open-ended discussions, creative thinking, and problem-solving.

Like the other second-grade classrooms, we ended the year reading *Charlotte's Web* by E.B. White. As Project-Based Learning (PBL) guided our teaching practice, we wanted students to engage in meaningful, hands-on work connected to the novel. PBL is an instructional approach where students learn by actively exploring real-world problems and challenges. Rather than memorizing isolated facts, students take on authentic tasks that require collaboration, problem-solving, and creativity.

For this project, our second-grade team designed an inquiry around farms, since the setting of *Charlotte's Web* naturally lent itself to this theme. Students researched how farms operate and worked together in groups to design their own farm. They began by creating square and rectangular enclosures (pens, sites, and stables) on poster board, which gave them a foundation of math and design. From there, creativity flourished as they turned flat drawing into 3-D displays. Toothpick fences framed their fields, small bushes and trees sprouted up, and barns and stables were carefully constructed. Of course, each farm included a thoughtful detail: a spider web for Charlotte woven delicately into the barn.

They beamed with delight at their farms, but they seemed to crave more. Taking note of the ability of my high-achieving class, I decided to have them calculate the area and perimeter of each of their animal habitats/enclosures. Before you question, "Are area and perimeter second grade standards?" No, they're not. In fact, area and perimeter were 3rd- and 4th-grade standards at the time.

I devoted some class time to area and perimeter for squares and rectangles, and when they mastered this, we worked together to calculate the area and perimeter of each of their animal enclosures. During our PBL Showcase night, when the kids shared their farms with their families, I noticed that the one thing they seemed most proud to share was the fact that they calculated area and perimeter. Parents thanked me for taking the time to challenge their children beyond the grade level standards and exclaimed that their kids often expressed being bored in school but felt that this project gave them a space to flourish. Like many elementary schools, the buzz of my students' farm projects began to circulate around the school.

The following day my principal was leading a tour of fellow school administrators and district leaders from a nearby state. The tour stopped by our "farms," and I heard her using our projects as an example of using PBL in the classroom. My principal called a few of my students and me into the hallway and invited a couple of students to explain our project to the group. Seemingly proud, my principal complimented the students' projects and my insight to challenge my students beyond the traditional scope and sequence of second grade.

At this time in my life, other peoples' opinions seemed to drive my self-acceptance, and I had finally earned the accolades and respect I had been seeking. Unfortunately, in my experience in elementary education, it seems that there is often a competition among teachers within a school. Sadly, in my personal experience as a teacher, I discovered that with success and praise comes those who want to tear you down. I'll never understand why this happens in public education, because it seems that when educators work together and build each other up, everyone benefits, especially the kids.

The following week one of my former first-grade teammates and leader of the Math Committee interrupted my class while I was teaching and asked me to step into the hallway. She asked me to explain the Charlotte's Web farm projects. A bit confused but also excited, I started rambling on and on about the farms, area, perimeter, and my high-achieving students. She interrupted me with a wave of her hand and proceeded to explain that it is not my place to teach 3rd- and 4th-grade math standards. This is the part where I if I could talk to my past self I would say,

> "Hey self, Tell Little Miss Math Police that it's not her place to stifle learning, creativity, and problem solving in a classroom where she has never set foot!"

Instead, I began defending my rationale for teaching area and perimeter to second graders.

"My students need more. They'll be more prepared in third grade. Why should I hold them back based on a one-size-fits-all set of standards determined by the state?"

She continued to exclaim that as the leader of the Math Committee it is her place to report me to administration for not understanding my job and deviating from my expected duties as a second-grade teacher.

I said, "Well before you report me, I think you should know that our principal added this fabulous PBL display to the tour of fellow school administrators and leaders, and during the tour she asked my students to explain what they learned including area and perimeter." I'm not going to lie y'all, I may have said this served with a bit of passive aggressive sass.

It felt good to have the backing of my principal, but having a fellow teacher accuse me of not performing my job as expected, and that yearly three out of four official rating, continued to frustrate and deflate me. Teaching is one of those careers where success is often determined by student data, parental praise, Teacher of the Year awards, and yes, teacher observation scores.

This praise may be more desired among extroverts like me; however, I suspect that most teachers appreciate feeling validated. As noted in the Undercover Recruiter, one of the best ways to help extroverts to succeed is to "praise them for what they do, because extroverts are always looking for stimulation from their surrounding environment."[1] I can't speak for all extroverted teachers; however, I craved validation, I wanted to stand out. I wanted to shine. I wanted to earn a respectable income. I wanted to finish my coffee hot, enjoy lunch without responding to emails or making copies. At the very least, I wanted the ability to use the restroom at my leisure.

Yet again I found myself questioning my decision to become a public-school teacher.

---

[1] "Strategies You Need to Know for Working with Extroverts." Undercover Recruiter, January 12, 2017. https://theundercoverrecruiter.com/work-with-extroverts-strategies/.

CHAPTER 4

Bless Your Heart

My aspirations were falling flat. Even my mother seemed to view my teaching career as lacking accomplishment. One summer I decided to visit my mom for the weekend. It was one of those moments where I left my wife and kids at home so I could enjoy some quality time with my mom one on one. It was a nice hot summer day, so she suggested we go to her neighborhood pool. She lived in one of those neighborhoods where all the residents must be fifty-five or older to purchase a home. I can totally see why a retired teacher would opt to live in a quiet kid-free neighborhood.

We packed some snacks, filled our water bottles, grabbed a couple of pool noodles, and headed to the pool. After baking in the sun for an hour or two, we decided to get into the pool. Bobbing up and down, the conversation was simple and light as we discussed the cold temperature of the pool, lunch plans, and what movie we should watch that evening. Just as we were deciding between pizza or burgers, a woman floated over and joined our conversation. Immediately, my mom introduces me as her daughter. We exchanged pleasantries, and the woman, whom I'll call Joan because I cannot remember her name, proceeded to tell my mom about her two children. I've been told that I am not the best listener, and I suppose that's true, because I cannot remember one thing about Joan's children. I recall that she was not necessarily bragging, but she made it known that her children were thriving and doing well. Following suit, my mom began talking about her four children.

I knew she would get to me last, because I am the youngest child and I had witnessed this dance many times before.

"My oldest. He lives in Ohio with his wife and two daughters. He's a corporate Vice President, and extremely successful. He worked his way up, and he is so successful that his wife can be a stay-at-home mom. I really miss him, but he has created such a beautiful life for himself in Ohio. He's such an inspiration, because he created such an amazing life although coming from a modest childhood."

"My next oldest, she's in education like me, but she is the Assistant-Superintendent at one of the state's most highly esteemed school districts. I never imagined how successful she would become when she decided to pursue education, but here she is likely on her way to becoming a superintendent. She's married with two amazing kids and has really made a name for herself in her community."

"My next youngest is happily married and living in rural Illinois. They have a dog, and she is trying to adjust to the cold midwestern winters. She too is doing quite well, but I am hoping that one day she and her husband come back home to Georgia. Not to brag, but she still holds many high school basketball records where she, her siblings, and I all graduated. Well all of us except Jere here (laughs and points to me) who changed high schools her senior year."

"And finally, this is my daughter, Jere, she's a 1st grade teacher in Atlanta at an inner-city school."

That was it. No mention of my wife, my kids, my dog, or the fact that I am adored by many at my school. My mom seemed to specifically note that I was teaching in an "inner-city" school, almost as if to say. "She teaches in one of those schools with challenging kids."

However, I want to clarify that from my point of view, I was thriving at that public school in Atlanta, GA. Earlier in my career, my mom seemed to hold my achievement as a teacher as a huge success, but here in this moment when compared to my siblings, I felt invisible. From later conversations, my mom explained that she was not comfortable mentioning my wife or kids, because she was nervous about peoples' reaction to my being married to a woman and having a family, but again, I have digressed.

The fellow noodler, bobbed up and down, looked at me and said, "You teach 'in' Atlanta. Well bless your heart."

This is where I must diverge and try to explain "Bless Your Heart" to all my non-Southern readers. Bless your heart can be used in many ways, but two distinct meanings seem to stand above all (compliments of Google Gemini):

1. Genuine Sympathy: It can express sincere sympathy, concern, or affection for someone, especially in times of hardship or misfortune.
2. Polite Condescension: However, it can also be used sarcastically or condescendingly, implying that the person is misguided, foolish, or in need of pity.

"The key is to pay attention to the speaker's tone of voice and the overall context of the conversation to determine the intended meaning."

From my point of view, the noodler's "bless your heart" seemed to say, "I feel bad for you for having to teach at this type of school."

Even though she did not explicitly say this, it was seemingly implied. Hoping to change her preconceived notion of teaching in Atlanta, I shared stories of my students and their families. I painted them in a positive light by sharing the facts. I explained that teaching is the one career that impacts all other careers. I clarified that I had intentionally sought out living and working in Atlanta, as I valued the diversity and opportunities of city-living, but it seemed the more I said the more desperate I sounded trying to convince them that my life was successful and notable.

Pool noodle lady and my mom began sharing a myriad of reasons why they prefer suburb living over city living but are thankful that people like me are willing to teach in city schools.

"Wait a minute! Why is it that I'm 'willing' to teach in the city? Why is teaching elementary school in Atlanta not as braggable as becoming a corporate executive, school leader, or holding high school records?" I thought to myself feeling overshadowed by my siblings' success.

You're probably saying that I put too much emphasis on external praise, and to that I say, you're right. Remember I mentioned earlier that extroverts like me often seek external praise, and let's just say that "bless your heart" was not the type of validation I longed for. I bobbed up and down feeling invisible and sorry for myself.

I want to take a moment and add, I know my mom was proud of me, and if she were alive today, she would be bragging to all her friends, pool noodle lady included, saying,

"My youngest daughter, Jere, wrote a book, gives keynote talks around the country, and has amassed many followers on social media, and thrives as a teacher and impacts many lives." My mom would even begin to outwardly accept my family and share, "My youngest daughter, Jere, lives in Atlanta with her wife and two kids." My mom had lived within the confines of her own upbringing and societal norms, but over time, she grew to understand that I was living the best life for me, and that is something many folks are unable to achieve.

When my mom passed away in early 2020, hundreds of people came to pay their respects at her funeral: family, friends, former colleagues, and countless former students, and the students all shared similar sentiments. "Your mom changed my life." "Thanks to your mom I went to college." "Your mom gave me the gift of a love for literature." "Your mom was my all-time favorite teacher."

My mom was more than "just a teacher," more than a "notable teacher." She was Teacher of the Year, she was a life-changer, someone who helped students thrive, and a teacher whose impact lives on for eternity. If you take one thing away from this book, please make it this: Teachers are not just teachers, and teaching is an admirable career, a braggable career, a successful career, and one in which parents of teachers should feel proud to share with their friends. For those who say, "Those who can't teach," I encourage you to say, "Those who teach, change the world." However, during that time in my life, I failed to understand the impact and greatness of teachers. I questioned my career choice and asked myself, *"Well, how did I get here?"*

CHAPTER 5

Longing for the Teacher I Needed as a Child

My path to becoming a teacher was not straightforward. As a matter of fact, it was more like a sailboat shifting in the wind, adjusting sails, sometimes drifting, sometimes speeding ahead. Becoming a teacher was never part of the plan. In fact, teaching was nowhere on my childhood bucket list. So, let's rewind to where it all didn't begin: my childhood, where the clues were hiding in plain sight probably under a pile of doodles and daydreams of skipping school until one day, I'd become the teacher I needed as a child.

I arrived in the world in 1972, fashionably late by three weeks and just an ounce shy of ten pounds. When I was born, I appeared to be a typical healthy baby. However, during my toddler years, my mom had difficulty potty training me. She began taking me to the doctor, and he suggested repeatedly that I was merely developing slowly and would achieve developmental milestones at my own pace. My mom knew something was off, as I was different as compared to my older three siblings all of whom she potty trained without any problems.

When I started kindergarten at a local church's half-day program, my mom gave my teacher a heads-up explaining that I was "developmentally delayed" as described by doctors; therefore, I'd be showing up to school in a diaper. She kindly let the teacher know that if I needed a change, the teacher could call my mom, and my mom would leave work, drive to school, and change me herself.

My kindergarten teacher expressed concern and sympathy as I struggled throughout the year with "potty-training." My father, on the other hand, suggested a good old-fashioned spanking to "fix this mess," but my mom stood her ground with him and said, "Something is wrong with her. I just know it."

By late kindergarten, things started getting more complicated. I wasn't just struggling with potty training anymore; I was getting hit with bladder and kidney infections. While other kids were learning to read "See Spot Run," my mom was taking me to yet another doctor's appointment.

It felt like my body was staging a rebellion, and no amount of cranberry juice or doctor visits seemed to make a lasting difference. The doctor visits kept coming, but by the time I entered first grade, I was still without a diagnosis.

Unfortunately, my first-grade teacher, Mrs. Kelman, didn't exactly radiate the same compassion as my kindergarten teacher. Where others had shown concern, she saw inconvenience. To her, it seemed that my challenges weren't medical or developmental, they were gross, disruptive, and frankly, a bit of a hassle. There was no medical report in my file, no 504 plan, nothing to clue the school in on what I was dealing with. Just a handful of doctors' notes suggesting that I was "delayed," and that I'd catch up eventually.

Spoiler alert: I didn't. Not in first grade, anyway.

That year marked the beginning of my aversion toward school, and I remember the specific shift vividly. It was bathroom break time, and in typical first-grade procedure, Mrs. Kelman, clipboard in hand, her voice sharp and no-nonsense, called us to line up. "Girls this way. Boys that way."

I followed the script. I went into the bathroom, took my place in the stall, and pretended to do what was expected of me. However, like always, I did not eliminate my bladder, but I knew the drill and acted accordingly. I washed my hands and walked out like all the other girls and took my place in line.

About five minutes after we returned from our bathroom break, Mrs. Kelman handed out a freshly printed purple ditto sheet filled with math problems. It was one of those ink-smudged masterpieces only vintage readers will truly appreciate. Naturally, the first thing I did was lean in and take a deep whiff of that unmistakable blueish-purple ink. (If you know, you know.) Then the race was on. I flew through those addition problems like a tiny math machine. Within two minutes, I was done. I glanced up at the K for Kangaroo, dangling slightly off the wall above the chalkboard like it was hanging on for dear life. The room buzzed with pencil scratching, eraser rubbing, and quiet frustration. Meanwhile, I soaked in the satisfying sound of Mrs. Kelman's sensible patent leather pumps click-clacking across the floor as she moved toward the back of the room.

Then I noticed something. She was walking… toward me.

A wave of hope washed over me. Maybe she's coming to give me a sticker for finishing first, I thought. But then reality slapped me in the face. Something told me this wasn't a gold-star moment. Mrs. Kelman stood over me, arms crossed, with that look teachers have when they think you've done something wrong. Her eyes were a dull kind of blue, and her mouth was pulled into a tight line, ready to say something I probably wouldn't like. Her hair was twisted into a no-nonsense bun, not a single strand out of place, kind of like her personality. Her face looked like it had spent years stuck in a permanent frown, and right now, it was aimed directly at me. "What is going on here?" she snapped. I stared straight ahead, pretending not to notice my soaked corduroy pants or the growing puddle under my desk. She wasn't buying it. "This!" she barked, pointing right at a puddle of urine surrounding my feet.

The room went silent for half a second before every single kid whipped around to watch the show, because if there's one thing kids love more than recess, it's watching someone else get in trouble. I shrugged sheepishly, sank further into my chair, and tried to disappear. Again, she barked, "Jere, I said what is this? Answer me now."

"I don't know," I whispered.

"Louder! I can't hear you!" she bellowed.

"I – I – I – don't know." I stuttered.

She asked why I didn't go to the bathroom with the rest of the class. I gave my usual answer: I didn't know. Apparently, that wasn't good enough. She launched into a full-on lecture, pointing out that she had personally walked the class to the restroom and watched me go in. In her mind, there was no logical explanation for why I had just peed all over the floor "like a dog," and of course, the class laughed.

She scribbled a note and sent me to the office, instructing me to call my mom to bring fresh clothes. As I stood up, she called out, "Jere, tell Mrs. Bridges at the front desk to send a janitor to clean up this disgusting mess, and by the way you won't be having recess today." I walked out of the classroom with my pants clinging to my legs, tears streaming down my face, while she stayed behind to give the rest of the class a bonus lecture on "how to use the bathroom like big kids."

And that, right there, was the beginning of my official hatred of school.

CHAPTER 6

The Hidden Disability

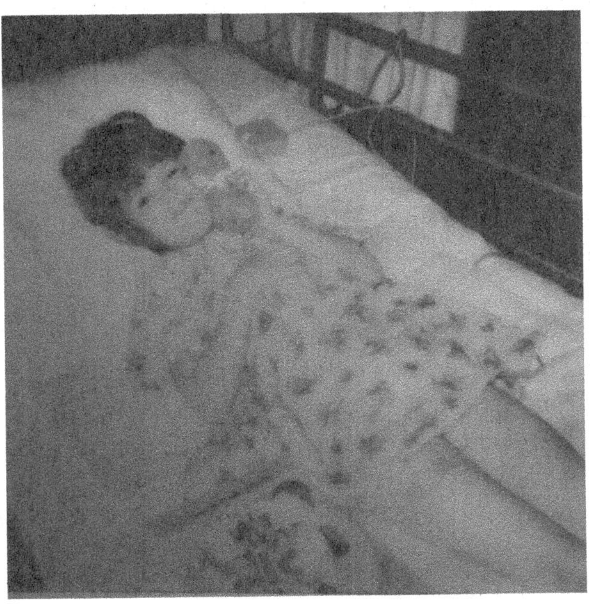

The bladder and kidney infections, the fevers, and the hospital visits played on repeat until that one severe kidney infection, halfway through my first-grade year, would land me in the hospital for nearly a week. Like all other school days, my mom woke up, made breakfast, and got us ready for school. As she was getting us ready for school, she noticed that once again I had a high fever. My siblings headed outside to catch the bus, and my mom gave me some Aspirin, put me in a cool bath, and laid me on the couch while she phoned the doctor. She immediately dropped the phone as I began to wildly hallucinate, sharing visions of my brother shining a flashlight toward my eyes, asking why my sister was climbing in and out of my ear, and chatting with my bus driver who I swore was in my living room delivering cupcakes. My fever had rapidly spiked, so my mom rushed me to the local hospital. The local doctors treated yet another kidney infection with IV antibiotics but suggested that I needed more acute medical care.

In the upcoming weeks, we took numerous trips an hour north to Egleston Hospital for Children's now known as Arthur. M. Blank Hospital (Children's Healthcare of Atlanta). Doctors were flown in from various places around the country, and finally I was diagnosed with spina bifida. Spina Bifida is the most common permanently disabling birth defect compatible with life, affecting about 166,000 people in the United States. My form, called Spina Bifida Occulta, wasn't visible at birth. It quietly revealed itself years later, when doctors discovered that the nerves between my brain and bladder weren't communicating properly. The result: a neurogenic, or paralyzed, bladder.

In other words, my brain tries to call my bladder to say, "Hey, you're full! Time to empty before bacteria overstay their welcome and cause an infection."

But the connection is fuzzy.

"Hello? What are you saying?" my bladder asks.

"I said empty yourself!" the brain yells back. "We'll get an infection if you don't!"

"Can you call me back later?"

"No! I've got other jobs to do besides managing urine!"

So the bladder hangs up without a care in the world, and before long, the brain starts shouting to everyone,

"All hands on deck! We have an infection because bladder refuses to do her job again!"

Unfortunately, my brain can't find another way to get the message through. The wires are crossed for good. So while I can feel the urge to go, I can't actually relieve myself without using a catheter—a quiet, constant reminder that my body has its own way of operating, and I've had to learn to listen to it rather than fight against it.

The doctors explained to my mom that I had some damaged nerves in my lower spinal cord, and some other nerves were attached to my spine. Doctors projected that by the time I reached 13 years old, the attached nerves would "possibly" sever, and I would eventually become paraplegic and require the use of a wheelchair. Doctors shared the risks of the surgery and explained that this type of surgery was rare and risky at the time and could potentially result in me immediately becoming paralyzed from the waist down during surgery. Fortunately, the surgery was a huge success. I spent a month in the hospital where I was adorned with visits, flowers, gifts, and a brand-new bicycle from my grandmother, Mama Bill.

And I'll never forget the care package Ms. Kelman sent complete with cheerful, handmade get-well cards and a glorious stack of purple-inked dittos that smelled just like elementary school nostalgia. I spent the following six months somewhat bedridden at home. While my friends were at school, I was at the kitchen table doing worksheets and reading books with my mom. I missed recess the most, but savored the fact that I no longer endured children teasing me about being the kid who peed her pants.

From that moment forward I never took the use of my legs nor the ability to pee while standing for granted. I use what's called self-intermittent catheterization. This is a process that involves inserting a sterile tube into the bladder every few hours. It would prevent future infections and give me back control over my bladder function. I have run three marathons, many ½ marathons, cycled across Colorado, earned a basketball scholarship, and now spend my evenings going on walks with my family and riding bikes with my wife and two kids around Atlanta.

I will forever be indebted to the incredible neurosurgeons and medical staff at Egleston Hospital. Their skill, compassion, and dedication not only saved my life, but they also inspired me to follow in their footsteps and pursue a life of healing as a brain surgeon. Very few children my age knew the word "neurology." Not only did I know the meaning of neurology (*a branch of medicine concerned especially with the structure, function, and diseases of the nervous system—Merriam Webster*), I lived it, and from that moment, I wanted to be a brain surgeon so that I too could change lives and help children in ways they never imagined possible.

I wish this was the pivotal moment in the story where my life began to take a turn for the better, and that time will come, but it won't come for many years. I wish I could say that children are sympathetic toward their classmates with a disability. I wish I could look back on my elementary school days in ways that were not defined by my disability. Yes, there were moments of happiness and success. For example, I won the local beauty pageant in fourth grade, I got third or fourth place in the school spelling bee, I usually won first place in the 100-yard dash on field day despite nearly losing the ability to walk. I remember all these memories fondly. But the day-to-day memories of my elementary school years were quite disappointing to say the least. When the teacher took the class to the restroom after lunch, I would head to the front office where I would meet my mom who would catheterize me for my daily restroom break. I always had an extra set of clothes on hand just in case, and I wore diapers until I was finally old enough to catheterize myself independently starting in the fifth grade. My disability, although I did not realize it at the time, defined me among my classmates.

I can't speak for everyone with a hidden disability, but my classmates seemingly did not see me as disabled as I was one of the most athletic kids in my school and I looked "normal." As a matter of fact, I too did not see myself as having a disability. I don't ever recall hearing the word "disability" in my home growing up, but I hated my disability. I felt weird. I felt invisible. I simply wanted to be normal. I did not want to be the stinky kid.

Nearly every day on the bus ride home my peers would continue to play, "Who's the Stinky Kid?" Imagine a circle of rowdy kids, laughing, counting, and randomly selecting and pointing at the "Stinky Kid" of the day. And every day I would join in hoping that today would be the day where I was not randomly selected, but that day never came. Somehow every day, I was randomly selected as the stinky kid. I would join in the laughter pretending that the kids were laughing with me and not at me, and every day I would walk off the bus and into my house. I would head straight to my bedroom where I would pretend to play and read to dolls, but instead I would simply cry.

As an adult, my mom would often reminisce with me and describe my younger self as a quiet child who loved playing "school" by reading to her dolls. I never had the heart to tell my mom that I was not a quiet child. I was an outgoing and energetic kid stifled by bullying, seeking an escape, a solitude, a place where I felt safe, and for me this place was my bedroom. My bedroom was the place where my stuffed animals and dolls accepted me for me. I am not attempting to get you, the reader, to feel sorry for me. I am simply sharing my experience. It is my hope that parents and/or educators reading this book may discover that you do not "know" your children/students as well as you think, because many of us mask and hide our feelings, sadness, or disability.

It never occurred to me to speak to a counselor about what I was going through. Sadness, shame, isolation, and wanting to belong all loomed over me while I presented myself as the smart, quick-witted, and happy child. Folks from my childhood such as family, peers, teachers, coaches, etc. may find my point of view surprising, because I had been taught to play the game. I grew up in a home where we don't "air our dirty laundry" with others. We don't share our private lives or feelings with others. I never recall anyone in my family telling me to keep my disability a secret, but something inside me felt a sense of secrecy. I would hold this secret tightly until my late 40s.

My life began to take a turn for the better by the time I started high school. I learned all the tricks to keep my disability hidden. I hid catheters in my shoes. I strategically waited to ask teachers for permission to go to the bathroom during times when the bathrooms would most likely be empty. I even convinced my mom not to file a section 504 medical plan at school.

> 504 plans are plans that schools make to give kids with disabilities the services and support they need to learn alongside their peers. 504 plans… can be used to help students with disabilities access education.[1]

Just as I was beginning to find my way, life decided to say, "let's humble you real quick."

---

[1] GeorgiaLegalAid.org | Free, Easy to Understand Legal Information and Resources. "What Should I Know About 504 Plans in Georgia?," April 13, 2022. https://www.georgialegalaid.org/resource/what-should-i-know-about-504-plans-in-georgia.

CHAPTER 7

Gay and Disabled

My confidence and self-acceptance began to grow as my athletic ability and silly sense of humor outshined my disability. In high school, I was a member of the state winning softball team, which came complete with a medal, a letterman's jacket, and immediate friends. As I entered my sophomore year of high school, things were looking up for me. I was fitting in, I received invites to a few parties, and I even managed to find a boyfriend. I was excited about having a boyfriend, because it meant doing boyfriend/girlfriend things like going to Applebee's, holding hands in the hallway, and having a date for the homecoming dance. But what I liked most was feeling normal and fitting in.

My mom was named Homecoming Queen at my high school many years ago, and then my older sister was named Homecoming Queen her senior year at the same school. "Maybe I too will have the honor of being named Homecoming Queen in a couple of years," I secretly wished.

My mom took me to JC Penney's on a mission to find a brand-new dress and shoes. I could hardly believe it. Me? New clothes? Not a single hand-me-down from my sisters in sight. I felt like I'd just won the jackpot. Life was good. At home, I spruced up my over-permed hair with enough hairspray to withstand a meteor strike.

At the dance, Chad and I swayed shyly in the dim light at least one foot between us. REO Speedwagon played on as Chad's Polo cologne engulfed the air. The carnation corsage bounced on my wrist, unsure of its purpose, just like the two of us. As we moved in hesitant circles, my mind kept drifting away to Leslie, my best friend.

You're having the most magical night of your life, and all you can think about is Leslie? She's not even here! Stop! This is gross. It's wrong! But I didn't stop. I couldn't stop. I did not understand my feelings, nor did I understand having "feelings" for a girl. However, this gayness seemed to have a mind of its own and crept into my life without warning, without direction, and without an explanation. It said, "Hey, Jere, I see you wearing those societal norms and going through the motions of small-town life, but you're not fooling anyone. Look around, you are not like the others. Yeah, your arms are wrapped around Chad as you dance the night away, but it just doesn't feel right, does it? Why don't you go ahead and tear down all those boy teen heartthrob posters you've plastered all over your bedroom walls. Admit it. You have a crush on Leslie. You like girls. You, my dear, are gay." I could not even imagine identifying as a lesbian.

In full transparency, the words *homosexual, gay,* or *lesbian* never crossed my mind or my lips, because at this time in the late 1980s, these were words used to describe people "living in sin." Homosexuals were people who had chosen a life of perversion. As someone who had grown up in the Southern Baptist church, and longing to fit in and be normal, I knew that thinking about my best friend in such a shameful way was not an option for me. For me there was nothing to choose, so I continued to live my life as expected until I didn't.

In the upcoming months my friendship with Leslie began to become a bit more romantic and intimate. It was new, exciting, and nurtured by shared secrets and a growing awareness of the feelings that lay beneath the surface. I am not sure if what we had was romantic love or a romantic friendship; however, I do remember a feeling of bliss when I was with Leslie. The feelings we shared were more than a friendship. Unfortunately, Leslie nor I knew how to exist in a closeted relationship, and we frequently exchanged love letters describing our feelings and our excitement to see each other again. My head was in the clouds, but feelings of bliss and teenage romance would all come crashing down with one phone call. Leslie phoned to tell me that her parents found our letters and that she was not allowed to see me anymore.

I sobbed, begged, and pleaded with her. Before long Leslie's mother took the phone from her. She described our letters as filthy and sinful and accused me of being a bad influence on her daughter, but it was what she said next that sent me into a deeper closet: "If you do not stay away from my daughter, I will share these disgusting letters with your mother," and just like that Leslie was gone. I could not risk my mother finding out about my "sinful" lifestyle.

Heart-broken and alone, I became utterly depressed. I had nowhere to turn. I didn't have a friend, sibling, parent, school counselor, or teacher with whom I could share my feelings. I remember my teachers and coaches teasing me and asking me why my best friend and I were no longer friends. One coach quipped, "Did you steal Leslie's boyfriend?" Like a typical teenager, I dodged the questions with shrugs or mumbles. I remember my mom asking if something was wrong. She could sense it, even when I tried to hide it, but I gave her the default teenage response, the one that kept everything safely tucked away, "I'm fine, Mom. Everything's fine."

But everything was not fine. My gayness was not going away, and I was dealing with my first broken heart. There was no Internet, no social media, no TV shows with gay characters. I had no gay or lesbian representation, so I decided to turn to the only trusted adult with whom I had access. I was enrolled in Health Education, which, of course, included the ever-so-awkward rite of passage known as sex education. The class was taught by none other than Coach Tate, a man better suited for a whistle and a football than diagrams of reproductive systems. There was something oddly surreal about learning about human anatomy and contraception from someone who yelled "hustle!" more than "hormones!" He'd stride into the classroom like it was game day, armed with outdated textbooks and an uncomfortable amount of enthusiasm for the word "abstinence," and for some reason, I thought this was the trusted adult I should ask about homosexuality.

After each lesson, Coach Tate would invite the class to write anonymous questions on index cards and place the cards in a shoe box. During the last five minutes of class, he would answer the questions. He encouraged us to ask any question no matter the content. This afforded us the opportunity to ask questions we were too shy or afraid to ask in front of our peers. One day I decided to ask, "Will you explain what it means to be homosexual?" I carefully shielded my card as I wrote the forbidden word h-o-m-o-s-e-x-u-a-l.

Coach Tate breezed through the cards, most of which asked, "Can you get pregnant if you _________?" Hormone raging teens were trying to determine what they could do with one another without resulting in a pregnancy. Finally, he pulled my gay card. I knew it was my card from the look of disgust in his eyes. He let out a snicker as he read, "Can you explain what it means to be homosexual?" As he flicked the card onto the floor he said, "I don't know whose sick joke this is, but homosexuality is a sin. God made Adam and Eve not Adam and Steve," and the class went wild. The laughter poured out into the hallway. Not wanting to be found out, I joined in the laughter, asking my classmate, "Who would ask such a crazy question?"

I felt so alone, longing to feel a connection with anyone: a friend, a teacher, a counselor, a sibling, a parent, anyone would do. Instead, I began to isolate myself in my bedroom and at school. Teachers and coaches told me that I should be more like my older siblings. My older siblings were popular, athletic, pretty, and normal. My mom encouraged me to, "Try harder to fit in. Spend more time on your appearance and you'll get another boyfriend." I so desperately wanted to fit in. However, I wanted to fit in being my true weird, quirky, authentic, disabled, and gay self, but that was not an option.

My mom began to suspect something as my depression loomed. One day she said, "Jere, sit down, we need to talk." I had no clue what she was about to say, but from my experience, no one ever shares good news when they ask you to sit down because they need to talk. As I unwrapped my Wendy's cheeseburger, she said, "Jere, I found all the letters between you and Leslie."

I was young, in love, and so naïve that it never occurred to me to discard the letters. I can't describe the disappointment in my mother's eyes or in the tone of her voice. I laid my cheeseburger down and played with a fry as my mom went on for what felt like an eternity trying to understand where she had gone wrong. How could someone who raised her children to make good choices and be "good kids" have a child who would explore such things with a girl. She began to analyze my childhood, my father's actions, her actions, my disability, my needing an emotional connection, etc.

My mother craved a reason and longed for a justification. She wanted someone to blame. I remember us talking about the fact that my parents divorcing early may have contributed to my "issues with boys," but what my mom failed to realize was that I did not have any issues with boys. As a matter of fact, I loved hanging out with boys, playing sports, and goofing off with them. I couldn't explain my feelings. I knew that I wanted to live a "normal life," but in my eyes a normal life seemed to involve dating girls. My mom needed answers, but answers were something I couldn't give her. So, I lied. Sobbing, I said, everything I needed to say to convince my mom that I had been led astray. I had made an egregious mistake, and that I was now on the right path. I assured my mom that I would not like any more girls, and I would pursue a boyfriend. I never finished that cheeseburger and fries, and I never told my mom that this moment crushed me and sent me into a greater depression. In my mom's defense, she truly thought she was protecting me, and in many ways, she did. Had I come out as gay in Sugar Hill, GA, in the late 1980s, my life possibly would have been ruined, and I never would have initiated *Operation Ungay*.

To execute my plan, I needed a fresh beginning, which meant changing schools. I figured if I could start fresh with people who had never met me, didn't suspect me of being gay, and didn't know I had a disability, it would give me the opportunity to start over and create a new life for myself. Halfway through my junior year of high school I presented the idea to my mom. I had sorted everything out. I explained that I could pretend to live at my dad's house in the neighboring school district, drive myself to a different school, and live happily ever after. As expected, my mom thought the idea was absurd. Looking back, I completely understand her hesitation to let me change schools, but that all changed when I had intensive jaw surgery the summer before my senior year.

I had jaw complications that necessitated a full-on surgical alignment. My mom scheduled my surgery during the summer so I would not miss school. In the months leading up to summer and my surgery, I started a weekend job at Lake Lanier Islands Beach and Water Park near my home. At this job I began making many friends at the school that I wanted to attend. I continued to plead with my mom about switching schools, but she was not too keen on the idea of me switching schools for my final year. "It's just too risky. It doesn't make sense," she would say.

My jaw surgery was a success, and I spent a day or two in the ICU before transferring to a general hospital room. On the next to last day during my hospital stint a group of five teenagers poured into my room with flowers, cards, gifts, and laughter. Surprised, my mom thought they were in the wrong room, because she did not know them. You see one thing about small towns: everybody knows everybody. My mom had attended high school with my classmates' parents. I had teachers who had taught my mom, which I do not recommend. Everyone was somehow connected, so my mom assuming the gaggle of teenagers had stumbled upon the wrong room made sense.

I could neither talk nor smile because my mouth was wired shut. As soon as I started writing to introduce my new friends to my mom on my little chalkboard, the giggly teens assured my mom that they knew me from Lake Lanier Islands. I informed my mom that the teens attended West Hall High School, the school I wanted to attend my senior year. After a nice visit, the teens left, and the following day I was discharged to recover at home. Once home, my mom asked me to sit down once again so we could talk, but this time she had good news. Apparently, people do share good news when they ask you to sit down and talk. My mom looked me in the eyes and her words would change my life forever, "Jere, I am so sorry I did not listen to you. Yes, you can change schools. Let's go ahead and start completing the paperwork."

I was elated. I asked my mom why she had changed her mind. She explained that I had grown up around the same kids, teachers, and coaches since I was in kindergarten. We played on the same teams, attended the same church, etc., and not one kid, teacher, church member, or coach called, sent a card, visited, or even inquired about my well-being. However, a group of kids I had recently met spent their Saturday afternoon hanging out with me in the hospital showering me with flowers, cards, and well wishes, and it was in that moment that she realized that support and friendship were not determined by years or proximity, they were determined by actions, kindness, support, and love. And just like that, the kindness of new friends and my mom's revelation and trust in my judgment would change my life forever.

CHAPTER 8

The Teacher Who Believed, the Coach Who Broke, and the Mom Who Fought Back

With only a few weeks left of summer, my mom and I scrambled to enroll me at my new school. Once on board, my mom was excited for my new adventures. Specifically, she was excited about the possibility of me having her college English professor. As a single mom of four kids, my mom made many sacrifices including postponing college until her four children were independent, and as the youngest, this meant she would start college during my high school years. My mom's college freshman English professor also taught English at my new high school. My mom had shared many stories about Mrs. Edwards from her engaging ways of lecturing, her attention to grammar, her love of literature, and her high expectations of her students. I told my mom I would take English with anyone if it meant leaving my old life behind.

My mom and I went to the new school where we were greeted by one of the high school counselors, and immediately my mom began inquiring about the possibility of me being enrolled in Mrs. Edwards's English class. The counselor thumbed through my transcripts and casually asked if I had plans to attend college.

"I don't know," I replied.

"What do you mean you don't know?" my mom quipped.

"I haven't really thought about my plans after high school. I guess I could go to college. Is it too late?"

"Absolutely not," the counselor replied, "but the only senior English course Mrs. Edwards teaches is AP English, and based on your transcripts, I don't believe AP English is the best course for you."

My mom was often described as a "sweet Southern lady," but many people didn't know that underneath that disposition was a strong and resilient woman who would do anything for her kids. She firmly believed that college would open doors beyond our small-town limits, and she was convinced that Mrs. Edwards's AP English class was key to getting me there. The school counselor repeatedly disagreed, but my mom wasn't one to back down. Finally, my mom proposed a compromise. She wanted to speak with Mrs. Edwards, and if she felt I wasn't a good fit, my mom promised to back off. Teachers reading this are probably assuming that my mom was one of "those parents." The type of helicopter parents who teachers dread having their child in their class. In fact, my mom was quite the opposite. She rarely inserted herself into any of my school challenges, but from her point of view, this was one of those life-changing opportunities, and she was not about to back down. The counselor, realizing defeat, agreed and directed my mom and me to Mrs. Edwards's classroom.

My mom tapped on the door and peeked inside. Mrs. Edwards was sitting on the floor, unwrapping stacks of textbooks and shelving them neatly at the back of the room. The moment she saw my mom, she sprang to her feet and greeted her with a warm hug.

"What are you doing here?" she asked, clearly surprised but happy.

Without missing a beat, my mom launched into our situation, wasting no time on sugar-coating. "This is my daughter, Jere," she said, motioning toward me. "Apparently, she decided she wants to go to college. . . about five minutes ago," and she gave me the kind of side-eyed look that only a mom can give. I didn't say a word. I just kept my eyes on my shoes, hoping that no one would notice how badly I wanted to be anywhere else while the grown-ups determined my academic destiny. My mom told Mrs. Edwards that I hadn't exactly been a shining star in high school, that my track record lacked the

AP sparkle, but I needed this class if I had any shot at making it in college. Mrs. Edwards paused, looking at me, then back at my mom. "Suzanne, you were one of my best college students ever," she said. "If your daughter is anything like you, I'm confident she'll do just fine in my class, but let me be clear; it won't be easy."

Mrs. Edwards handed me three books: *Animal Farm, Invisible Man*, and *Jane Eyre*. "These are the required summer reading books for AP English," she said. "We're starting with *Animal Farm*, so make sure you read that one before school starts." I cracked open *Animal Farm* on the way home. I was attempting to act like the kind of student who actually enjoys summer reading, but a few pages in, I started to panic.

"Uh, Mom?" I said, eyes still glued to the page. "I don't think this is the right book."

She glanced at me. "Why not? Mrs. Edwards gave it to you herself."

"Well, she said it was a political fable, but this is clearly a cute little story about some talking farm animals. It's kind of like *Charlotte's Web*. It's not about politics and government," and that was the moment I seriously questioned whether signing up for AP English had been a massive mistake. Before we even made it home, my mom swung by the local bookstore and bought me a copy of the *CliffsNotes* for all three books. *CliffsNotes* are those little yellow books filled with cheat-sheet level insight and just enough analysis to make you sound halfway prepared. That day, I officially entered the world of allegorical fiction. I quickly discovered that *Animal Farm* was not about pigs with personality; it was about politics, power, and revolution, and just like that, AP English was about to get real.

School started, and I immediately reconnected with the friends I had made at my summer water-park job. I checked in with the girls' basketball coach to let him know I was serious about trying out for the varsity team. My confidence even soared as I walked into AP English ready to use my new word: *allegory*. I was also prepared to use "satire" and "utopia" during classroom discussions, but the second class began, I realized I had seriously underestimated the playing field. These kids weren't just smart; they were in a league of their own. Valedictorian. Salutatorian. Band kids who could recite Shakespeare. Theater kids who analyzed characters for fun, and bookworms who treated literature analysis as a hobby. Meanwhile, I was the athlete and basketball hopeful who maybe if I hustled hard enough, I could land a scholarship to a small college. I felt lost and out of place and, quite honestly, downright dumb. I didn't belong in AP English, and not among these academic powerhouses. That's what I believed, but I had no clue that Mrs. Edwards was about to reroute everything I thought I knew about myself.

A few weeks into the school year I went to Mrs. Edwards's room before school. I walked in head hanging low, and sheepishly said, "Mrs. Edwards I need to get out of your AP English class immediately," and when she asked why, I replied, "I need to be in the class with the regular kids." Mrs. Edwards asked me to explain myself, and I informed her that my peers in the AP English class had been reading books, she laughed and said, "Yeah that's what we do in AP English." I said, "No! You're not getting the whole picture. These kids read books that you're not even assigning, while I'm over here dribbling a basketball trying to figure out Janet Jackson's latest moves." Mrs. Edwards lowered her reading glasses, looked me in the eyes and said, "Jere, I see potential in you, and I believe you're capable of incredible things. You might not see it yet, but trust me, it's there. I'm here to remind you, challenge you, and push you to believe in yourself the way I do." Trusting Mrs. Edwards, I agreed, not that I had a choice, to remain in AP English although I felt as if I did not belong with the other AP kids.

However, unlike my previous school experiences, these "smart, nerdy, quirky" kids were kind and welcoming. Instead of ridiculing me for being different, one girl offered to help me understand the text after school, another boy offered to help me study for tests, and within just a few short weeks, I discovered a whole new world. I would never perform at the level of my classmates, but Mrs. Edwards and my classmates saw something in me that I did not see in myself. They saw someone who was late to the game, but eager to attend college. I would later fail my AP English exam, but taking this class would lay the foundation that would eventually earn me a college degree, three graduate degrees, and a journey to be a teacher just like Mrs. Edwards.

Life was beginning to fall into place. I was making new friends, keeping up in my classes, and the best part? I was doing all of it as me and not as someone's younger sibling, not as anyone's shadow, and not as a watered-down version of what I thought I should be. For once, I didn't have to explain myself. I still kept my disability and queerness tucked away, because I just wanted to blend in and feel normal. I simply wanted to belong, and for the first time in a long time, I did.

Basketball season started, and things were looking good. The coach seemed glad to have me on the team. I wasn't the star player or anything, but I could hold my own. I figured if I worked hard, basketball might help me get into college without taking on a ton of debt, but two weeks before our first game everything unraveled. The coach called me into his office, and I could immediately tell that he was about to deliver some bad news.

"I have some bad news," he said, hesitating. "Your basketball coach from your old school called the Georgia High School Association. He reported you as ineligible, and said you don't technically live with your dad, even though your school records say you do. He claims that you still live with your mom, which is not in our school district. Therefore, you're not eligible to play basketball here or even attend our school."

My stomach dropped. "Wait, what? How does he know where I live? He doesn't live anywhere near me?"

My coach sighed. "Apparently, he has been driving by your mom's house every morning before school. He says he sees your car in the driveway."

I stared at him. "Why is he driving by my house? Why does he care where I attend school? This makes no sense." My mind began to drift back to playing basketball for my former coach.

Back at my old school, basketball was more discouraging than empowering. My coach barely played me, no matter how hard I worked in practice. Look, I get it. It's sports. Not everyone gets to be on the court all the time. Sometimes you're just not the right fit for the game plan, or someone else is having a better week, but this seemed different. My coach told me on several occasions that I should be more like my older sisters. He told me that I had the worst attitude on the team and that I'd never amount to anything. When someone in a position of authority tells you you're not good enough often enough, it starts to settle in as truth. However, what I didn't know then was that his words said more about him than they did about me. I'll never understand why he seemed to have a vendetta about me trying to pursue a better quality of life. Maybe he truly believed I was doing something unethical; however, from my point of view, I was simply trying to position myself in a way to help me achieve my goals.

"I know," he said, looking genuinely upset. "I really hate this, but until the State Association makes a decision, you can't practice with us."

I drove home to the very house I technically wasn't supposed to be living in, at least according to the school records. I sat on the couch in that familiar living room, trying to hold myself together while the clock ticked toward my mom's usual return from her evening college class. The weight of everything pressed down on me, and I just sat there, stewing in frustration and disbelief, rehearsing how I was going to tell my mom what happened without completely falling apart. The second she walked through the door, all that rehearsing went out the window and I completely unraveled. I broke down in tears, words spilling out between sobs as I told her what my coach had said, how I could not play basketball at my new school, and I may have to return to my old school unless I officially move in with my father, which was not an option for reasons I choose not to share.

For a moment, my mom just sat there, as if trying to understand how a coach she once highly revered, who had coached my older sisters with such care, could be the same man now pulling strings to derail my future. She was livid and heartbroken, but more than anything, she was disappointed. She was disappointed in the coach she had once respected. How was this the same man she had trusted with all three of her daughters? Sure, he had wins under his belt, and championship banners hung in the gym. He had a reputation as a tough but respected coach and leader in the community, but in that moment, in our small living room, none of that mattered. He may have been a celebrated coach on the court, but from my point of view he was merely someone standing in the way of my future success. To him it may have been business as usual. However, it was life-changing for me, and my mom was not about to let him ruin my dreams.

She was fully prepared to do whatever she needed to do to help me stay at my new school. She called my dad and as soon as he heard what had happened, he was ready to help. He owned a dump trucking company, and by the next morning, he had hauled a full load of gravel to my mom's house. By noon, he had created a makeshift parking pad behind my mom's house so I could tuck my car out of sight from any potential spies. If my former coach still felt like playing neighborhood watch, he wasn't going to find anything in the driveway this time. My dad was a country man who was not about to let his kid get pushed around regardless of rules and regulations.

Next, my mom got on the phone with an old friend who just so happened to be the principal of my former high school. They were childhood friends, and lucky for me, they were still on good terms. She explained the situation and asked if he would be willing to write a letter to the Georgia High School Association confirming that I had left the school on positive terms. Without hesitation, he said yes, and by the end of the day we had the letter in hand ready to submit to the Georgia High School Association.

Then came the legal piece. My mom reached out to yet another high school friend who was an attorney. She explained the issue and asked for help drafting up some documentation that showed my parents shared joint custody, and that I was officially living with my dad. Her friend agreed right away. She understood the stakes, but she wanted to help, and within hours, she had the paperwork ready to go. With all the pieces in place, we filed an appeal with the State Association. I didn't know what to expect. I tried not to get my hopes up, but deep down, I was clinging to the possibility that this whole mess could be made right.

A week later, I was cleared. I could play basketball at my new school. It wasn't just a win for me. It was a win for every student who has ever been unfairly held back by technicalities or politics or adults who forgot that kids deserve second chances. It was a reminder that sometimes, the best kind of teamwork doesn't happen on the court, it happens at the kitchen table, over phone calls, through gravel deliveries, and in the quiet determination of parents who refuse to give up on their child's dream.

That experience, and so many others, brought me here. I can't say for sure how my life would've unfolded if Mrs. Edwards had listened to the school counselor who recommended I take general English instead of AP. I can't predict who I'd be if she had nodded politely and shuffled me into a less challenging class, but what I do know is that simply being in that AP English class changed my life. It gave me the confidence to believe in myself, the reassurance that I belonged, and the clarity to see a future I'd never imagined possible.

CHAPTER 9

We're Just Getting Started

Looking back, I realize that teachers like Mrs. Edwards did more than just show up and teach a subject. She wasn't just the person who handed out essays and gave grades. Mrs. Edwards saw her students and noticed the ones who were trying, the ones who were struggling, and the ones who didn't yet believe in themselves. She pushed us in a way that felt personal, like she knew what we were capable of even when we didn't. That kind of support stays with you, and it certainly stuck with me. Because of teachers like Mrs. Edwards, I know that I too can make a difference in the lives of the students I teach.

I want to be the kind of teacher students remember not just for what I taught, but for how I made them feel. I want my classroom to be a place where every student walks in knowing they matter, where they don't have to hide who they are just to fit in. I want my students to believe they're smart, capable, and worth investing in, no matter what their test scores say, what their home life looks like, or how many times they've been underestimated. I want to push them gently outside their comfort zones and then cheer them on when they realize they're capable of more than they thought. I want learning to feel exciting and something they get to do, not something they're forced to do.

Teaching changed when I stopped waiting for the perfect plan and started designing my own journey. Grandma's words echo in my mind, especially during those moments when the passion fades or when the challenges of the job feel too heavy to carry alone. That advice has stuck with me, guiding me through some of the hardest parts of my career and reminding me to make the work my own.

For someone like me, an extrovert who thrives on energy and connection, teaching can sometimes feel like a tug-of-war between giving everything to your students and still needing reassurance that you're doing enough. I used to spend so much time seeking validation from all the adults around me: family members, coworkers, administrators. I wanted to hear that I was good at this, that I was making a difference, that I was seen, but eventually, I realized that if I wanted to thrive, I had to stop measuring my worth by the opinions of others and start focusing on what really mattered: the kids.

So, I made a choice, and I decided to become the kind of teacher I needed as a child. I leaned into my fun, quirky, and even a little unpredictable nature in the best way imaginable. I brought that energy into the classroom. I made space for celebration, for joy, for high expectations wrapped in warmth. I stopped waiting for permission to be the teacher I knew I could be and simply began to celebrate me. I became the kind of teacher who notices every student and not just the ones who speak up the most or earn the highest scores. I chose not to define kids by a single behavior, a rough day, or one disappointing test. Instead, I looked for their strengths, even when they were buried beneath challenges. Where others saw problems, I made a point to see potential. I celebrated my students for exactly who they were, while still encouraging them to stretch and grow. I became the teacher who stands up for what's right, who speaks up when it matters, and who builds relationships that extend far beyond the classroom walls. More than anything, I wanted my students to feel truly seen, genuinely valued, and deeply remembered. And somewhere along the way, I stopped searching for external validation. The joy and purpose I had been looking for was already there in the laughter of my students, in the quiet breakthroughs, in the chaos of a classroom that feels like home. I designed my journey, and it turns out, my journey makes a difference in my students.

It's important to remember that some of the most meaningful lessons we teach won't come from a textbook or a carefully crafted lesson plan. They won't always happen during a scheduled period or even inside the classroom at all. Sometimes, the most powerful moments unfold when we least expect them. A casual conversation during recess about what's fair can spark a meaningful dialogue about justice and empathy. A spilled juice box in the cafeteria might look like a mess, but with the right approach, it becomes a chance to teach responsibility, problem-solving, and grace under pressure. Meaningful conversations with students can often provide context, connection, and real-world meaning that no worksheet could ever replicate.

Teaching the Whole Child

As teachers, our impact reaches far beyond our lesson plans. It lives in the way we respond to challenges, the way we model kindness and resilience, and the way we create space for questions that don't always have easy answers. Learning happens when students see that education is not just about standards or scores, but about navigating life, understanding others, and growing as people. When we embrace those unexpected teachable moments and see them as valuable parts of the learning journey, we give our students more than knowledge; we give them wisdom. We help them see that learning isn't just something they do for a grade; it's something they carry with them and live every day. Celebrating the whole child acknowledges that success is not solely measured by test scores but also by the development of character, empathy, and confidence. In doing so, teachers empower students to become well-rounded individuals prepared for both academic and life challenges.

Imagine a classroom where curiosity is encouraged just as much as getting the right answer. Picture a space where skills like resilience, creativity, and kindness are woven into each day even if they don't appear on the official lesson plan. When we make emotional intelligence and social growth part of our teaching, we're doing more than covering content, we're helping students develop the tools they'll need long after they leave our classrooms. By creating that kind of environment, we're not just setting students up to succeed in school, we're preparing them for life beyond it. We're helping them build confidence, empathy, and the ability to face challenges with a sense of possibility, and in doing so, we're helping them navigate the real world with heart and courage.

My school requires me to write two professional goals every year, and one year I decided to write a goal aligned with "celebrating the whole child," because I was really beginning to lean into the value of building relationships with students. Knowing that I work at a data-driven school, I was careful to include a goal centered around data and achievement. We are required to include a data-driven goal, but I wanted to write a goal about building relationships with students. For my second goal I wrote, "I strive to get to know students who do not qualify for gifted education services." I wrote this goal because in my experience I have discovered that many of us teachers get so busy with our students and classroom demands that we don't have the opportunity to get to know students beyond our classroom walls. As a gifted education teacher, I did not want to be the teacher "who only cares about students if they qualify for gifted education services."

My assistant principal scheduled my goal-setting meeting with me and explained that I could only submit "data-driven goals" in the district's teacher evaluation platform. I shared my disappointment with her, but she explained that this was one of those things "above her paygrade," and I complied. I'm not saying that data-driven goals have zero purpose in schools. I use data every day to see how my students have progressed and what they have achieved. However, I believe it's just as important to give teachers the space to set goals that reflect their personal growth and teaching values and not just those tied to data or test scores. I asked her advice for a data-driven goal, and I typed exactly what she said. To this day, I don't remember if I met my data driven goal, but in my heart, I continued to pursue my initial goal of "getting to know students," because I believe in making a difference in students' lives regardless of their gifted eligibility status, and my initial goal would lead to arguably one of the greatest overall impacts I would ever have on a student.

Jere and Jeri

One morning, I was strolling down the hallway on my way to the copy room when something unexpected caught my attention.

I overheard a teacher scolding a third grader. I have no idea what this little girl had done, but the teacher's tone was harsh enough to make me slightly pause mid-step. As I turned my head, I heard the teacher yell out, "Jeri!" I stopped in my tracks, and thought to myself, "Did she just say Jeri? There's no way." I rarely meet anyone with my name, especially children, no matter how it's spelled. I smiled to myself and kept walking, but I made a mental note: *Jeri.*

The following day I saw Jeri walking down the hall, and I immediately stopped her and said, "Oh my gosh is your name really Jeri?" She seemed a bit annoyed, looked up, smirked, and said, "Yeah, why are you asking?" I said you're not going to believe this, but my name is also Jere, but I spell mine J-e-r-e. She said, "No way! Can I call you Jere?" I said, "I'll make a deal with you," "How about you call me Ms. Jere?" "Deal," she replied.

Later that day, as her class made their way down the hallway, I stood by my door, watching the students pass. Out of the blue, Jeri and I spotted each other. Her eyes lit up, and with a big grin, she waved enthusiastically and called out, "What's up, Ms. Jere?" Several heads turned at once. Her teacher, who had no idea about our recent interaction, stared at Jeri in confusion. Raising an eyebrow, she asked sharply, "What did you just call Ms. Chang?" For a split second, there was an awkward silence hanging in the air, and I could see Jeri hesitate, unsure if she had just gotten herself into trouble yet again. I laughed and said, "It's okay! I gave Jeri permission to call me Ms. Jere." Her teacher looked at me, still puzzled, so I explained further. "It turns out Jeri and I share the same first name, but it's spelled differently, so I told her that she has permission to call me Ms. Jere." Jeri's teacher laughed and so did a few of the students. Jeri gave me a quick fist-bump as her teacher told the class to hurry along. Jeri turned, smiled, and in that moment, I knew that I felt as if I had made the right decision to trust my instincts and set a goal that impacts students well beyond data.

A few weeks passed, and Jeri and I kept building our little hallway friendship. Every time we crossed paths, we exchanged high fives, fist bumps, and cheerful "what's up" greetings. It became our tradition, a small but joyful moment that always made me smile. At the time, I thought it was just a fun and simple connection. I had no idea the real impact it was making on her.

Then came the day that changed everything. I was sitting at my desk during my lunch break when my classroom phone rang. I picked it up and heard the school counselor's voice on the other end. She started by asking if I knew a student named Jeri, and before I could even answer, she launched into an explanation. Jeri had gotten into a "scuffle" at recess. There had been some kind of ongoing conflict with another student, and while the administration did not want to suspend her, they also needed to find a way to address the situation before it escalated further. The counselor explained that she had been working with Jeri, trying everything she could think of to get her to open up, but Jeri was angry and closed off.

The counselor told me that Jeri was sitting in her office with her arms crossed and refusing to talk until the counselor said, "Look, Jeri, I am doing everything I can to keep you from being suspended, but you have got to help me help you. Is there anyone in this school you would be willing to talk to?" to which Jeri apparently responded, "Yeah. I'll talk to Ms. Jere." The counselor asked Jeri to describe Ms. Jere, because as far as she was concerned, there was no one at the school named Ms. Jere. Jeri began describing me in detail and finally the counselor laughed and said, "Are you talking about Ms. Chang?" Jeri thought for a second and said, "I don't know her teacher name, but she told me I could call her Ms. Jere."

Hearing the story unfold over the phone, I could not help but grin. The counselor asked if she could bring Jeri down to my room to talk, and of course, I said yes. Minutes later, they arrived. I pulled up a chair, set aside the rest of my lunch, and spent the remainder of my break sitting with Jeri and the counselor. Jeri opened up slowly, talking about the conflict she had with the other student. She was still hurt and frustrated, but with a little patience, a few jokes, and a lot of listening, she finally began to share what had been weighing on her. That day showed me something important. What I thought was just a few high fives and smiles was much more. It made a difference in Jeri's life. Sometimes the smallest moment like a wave, a nickname, or just a random act of kindness can mean the world to a student who needs someone in their corner.

With the support of Jeri's teacher and the administration, we created a plan. When Jeri felt a need to talk to a trusted adult, she would ask to be excused and come to my classroom and chat with me for a bit, and if I was teaching a class, Jeri would grab a book or magazine from my back table and sit in a safe space in my classroom until she felt comfortable returning to class. Eventually, I would invite Jeri to serve as my "co-teacher" if I was teaching first grade. During my planning period or lunch break, Jeri and I would chat about her challenges or play chess. Basically, I gave Jeri a space to escape for a few minutes when needed. I understand that this plan may not work in every school or with every child; however, sometimes the best plan is no plan at all. A few weeks later my classroom phone rang once again, and I was surprised when I heard who was on the other end.

"Hi, this is Jeri's mother," she said.

Immediately, my stomach tightened. My mind raced, and I braced myself for what I thought was coming. Was she upset that I had been meeting with her daughter during lunch breaks? Was she going to accuse me of overstepping? Even though every part of me knew my intentions had been good, I could not help but worry. After all, sometimes in education, it seems that no good deed goes unpunished. I took a deep breath and prepared to defend myself, but instead of anger, what I heard next caught me completely off guard.

"Thank you," she said, her voice full of emotion. "Thank you, Ms. Chang, for being a part of my daughter's village." She went on to explain that she, too, was an educator. She worked at a different school, and she knew firsthand how much it meant when a teacher took the time to truly see a child. She told me that she valued the teachers who made an impact, who took the extra moments to lift a student up, and that she was deeply grateful I had become one of those people for her daughter.

I assured her that her daughter was in good hands, and that it had been my joy, not my burden, to be a part of Jeri's journey, and that I too rely on educators to be a part of my village for my children. Remembering this call reminds me that teaching is never just about lessons and homework. It is about building a village. It is about standing alongside families and helping raise confident, resilient, and hopeful young people.

I may never fully know the specific impact I had on Jeri. However, I am certain that no test, dataset, or statistic can truly measure the difference I made in her life. It is often said that teachers should "stick to teaching" and avoid "indoctrinating our children." According to the Merriam-Webster Dictionary, the word *indoctrinate* means "to teach (someone) to fully accept the ideas, beliefs, and opinions of a particular group and to not consider other ideas, opinions, and beliefs." I wish these folks knew that teachers are not trying to indoctrinate children. We are simply trying to celebrate all children regardless of our differences.

Did I deviate from the third-grade standards? Yes. Was Jeri a student of mine? No, but according to Deleon Gray in a 2021 interview with J. Bowen, "A sense of belonging at school means feeling a sense of acceptance, respect, inclusion and support in a learning environment." Gray goes on to say, "students who feel a sense of belonging at school are typically more energized, more likely to spend time on-task and return to activities, and more likely to choose to be in the school environment."[1] While I cannot predict Jeri's future, I wholeheartedly believe that the collaboration among administrators and staff at my school, along with the trust placed in us by Jeri's mother, greatly contributed to her overall well-being and success throughout the remainder of her elementary school years.

The Lessons We Don't Grade: Mental Health at School

Unfortunately, many schools remain ill-equipped to support students like Jeri beyond the traditional scope of the classroom. In a 2023 article by DePaoli and McCombs, numerous studies highlight the positive impact that school counselors have on various aspects of student and school well-being. Counselors play a critical role in reducing disciplinary incidents and fostering academic achievement. Despite these benefits, the capacity of schools to meet the mental health needs of students remains limited. On average, public schools employ only one counselor for every 408 students and one school psychologist for every 1,127 students. These ratios significantly

---

[1] Bowen, Janine. "Why Is It Important for Students to Feel a Sense of Belonging at School? 'Students Choose to Be in Environments That Make Them Feel a Sense of Fit,' Says Associate Professor DeLeon Gray | College of Education News." *College of Education News*, October 21, 2021. https://ced.ncsu.edu/news/2021/10/21/why-is-it-important-for-students-to-feel-a-sense-of-belonging-at-school-students-choose-to-be-in-environments-that-make-them-feel-a-sense-of-fit-says-associate-professor-deleon-gra/.

exceed the recommended standards for mental health support in schools, underscoring a substantial gap in available services. Moreover, only 42% of schools currently provide mental health treatment services, demonstrating an urgent need for expanded resources and staffing to adequately address the growing mental health concerns among students.[2]

In a 2024 blog post, the Council for Exceptional Children outlined several strategies for schools to improve the mental health of students. These strategies include providing students with a safe space, recognizing signs of emotional distress, collaborating closely with colleagues, involving parents and guardians in the support process, and building positive relationships with students by "genuinely showing interest, care, and respect for each individual and going out of your way to get to know students' interests and strengths."[3]

Teaching Beyond the Data

While these practices are critical, they also point to a larger truth about education: schools must prioritize the development of the whole child and not just their academic performance. Focusing exclusively on data, test scores, and standardized outcomes overlooks the essential emotional, social, and psychological needs that contribute to a student's overall success and well-being. Students are not just numbers on a spreadsheet; they are unique individuals with diverse backgrounds, aspirations, challenges, and strengths. By investing in counseling services, mental health supports, community partnerships, and relational teaching practices, schools send a powerful message: a student's worth is not determined by their test scores but by their humanity. True success is cultivated when we nurture both the mind and the heart. As educators, we have a profound responsibility to create spaces where every child can thrive not only as a learner but also as a person.

---

[2] Learning Policy Institute. "Safe Schools, Thriving Students: What We Know About Creating Safe and Supportive Schools," September 27, 2023. https://learningpolicyin stitute.org/product/safe-schools-thriving-students-brief.

[3] Council for Exceptional Children. "A Guide for Teachers: How to Improve Mental Health in School," n.d. https://exceptionalchildren.org/blog/guide-teachers-how-improve-mental-health-school.

I often wonder what school would have been like for me if I had more teachers like me or Mrs. Edwards? What if my teachers saw a kid trying to hide her disability and gayness by trying to fit in and feel normal? Jeri reminded me why I keep showing up. It inspires me to persevere through the hard days, the paperwork, the changing mandates, and the angry parents.

We do not need capes, or badges, or magic wands (although a magic wand would really come in handy on payday). We need heart. We need humor. We need the stubborn belief that even when it feels like nothing is changing, we are still making a difference one conversation, one encouragement, or random act of kindness at a time. Teachers are not just preparing students for the next test. We are preparing them for life, and for the moments when life calls for resilience, creativity, kindness, and courage.

A Message to You

So, to every teacher out there, thank you! Thank you for showing up every day with heart, humor, patience, and grit. Thank you for being more than instructors, for being encouragers, listeners, problem-solvers, and role-models. Thank you for those quiet words of encouragement, the second chances, the extra smiles, and the tough conversations handled with care. We are doing some of the most important work there is, even when it feels like no one is listening. Keep going. We are making a difference, and the world is better because of us. You are seen. You are valued, and you are needed now more than ever. As we move into the next part of this journey, remember education is not just about filling minds. It is about filling hearts. It is about lighting the way forward, even on the days when your own path feels a little dim. The work you are doing matters. You matter, and we are just getting started.

PART II

The Strategies That Inspire Me

Introduction

People often ask how I've not only survived but managed to actually enjoy teaching for so many years. I usually just smile, shrug like it's no big deal, and say, "Have fun and keep it simple," right? However, if you've spent any time in a classroom lately, you know it's not always that easy. Between the endless demands, the micromanagement, the constantly shifting policies, and the ever-popular complaint about "kids these days," it's no wonder so many teachers are exhausted, disheartened, or questioning how much longer they can hang on.

Yet here's the thing: when the classroom door swings shut and the noise of the outside world finally fades away, something magical can happen. In that quiet and sacred (as well as wild and boisterous) space, teaching stops feeling like a job and starts feeling more like a journey even when it's a three-ring circus. Danish philosopher Søren Kierkegaard once said, "What the teacher is, is more important than what he (or she) teaches," and after years of living and breathing this work, I believe he is absolutely right. Students won't always remember the exact lessons you taught, or the Pinterest classroom that you gave up part of your summer decorating, but they will always remember you.

Teaching is the only profession that shapes every other profession out there. Behind every doctor in the operating room, every artist painting a masterpiece, every astronaut floating through space, and every musician selling out arenas, there was a teacher who helped light that first spark. It does not always happen with some grand, life-changing moment either. Sometimes it looks like a parent patiently teaching their child how to clean their room without stuffing everything under the bed. Other times it looks like a mentor coaching future legends like Simone Biles, Nelson Mandela, Dr. Martin Luther King Jr., Taylor Swift, Marie Curie, or Neil Armstrong. Teachers are everywhere, quietly working behind the scenes, fueling greatness.

Picture a world without Johannes Gutenberg. Not ringing a bell? He invented the printing press. Without him, books would have possibly stayed rare, hand-copied treasures locked away in monasteries and castles, and without mass-produced books, chances are you would not be sitting here reading this right now. Unless, of course, you are on a digital copy. Then you have Michael Hart to thank, the man who kicked off the idea of e-books back in 1971, long before anyone even dreamed of Wi-Fi or tablets. The point is, behind every great invention, movement, performance, or discovery, there was someone who took the time to teach. Someone who believed that knowledge was not meant to be hoarded, but shared, and that someone is you.

Real Talk

How do we block out all the noise that creeps into our classrooms and tries to throw us off track? It is easy to sit here in this coffee shop, wrapped in the cozy glow of a week-long break, sipping something warm, and convincing myself that teaching is pure magic. The smell of roasted coffee beans, the soft jazz humming in the background, and the fact that no one is asking me if they can go to the bathroom for the fifth time during a five-minute lesson all make it feel like anything is possible. But then Monday shows up. The alarm sounds and the reality of drinking my coffee at the coffee shop fades. You walk into your classroom and there it all is, waiting for you: the endless expectations, the paperwork that somehow multiplies overnight, the meetings that could have been emails, and the ever-dwindling list of resources you are supposed to stretch into a masterpiece, and then the students come rolling in with their broken uncharged Chromebooks, dropping water bottles, asking, "What are we doing today?"

This is when the real test hits you. Not the "sharpen-your-pencil" or charge-your-Chromebook kind, but the pop quiz life throws at you when you are running on fumes and cafeteria pizza. It is the test of whether you can find even a tiny shred of joy when you feel stressed out, tired, and hopeless.

Finding the magic in teaching is not about chasing the perfect days. It is about learning how to spot it buried under the chaos, the noise, and the questionable smells coming from the back of the room. Some days I want to fake my own kidnapping and other days I know I am changing the world one kid at a time. If you have ever wondered whether the long days and unseen effort truly matter, you're not alone. This next part is for you. For the teacher who is tired, a little worn down, but still hanging on to the hope that it does not have to feel like this forever. It is about finding the fun again, but not ignoring how hard it gets.

At the beginning of each chapter in Part II you'll find a *Brain Pleaser*. This is a simple question to spark curiosity and reflection. Let the questions sit with you as you read and notice how your answers evolve along the way. Ahead, you will find real stories, real strategies, and a whole lot of real talk about how to survive teaching without losing yourself along the way. Who knows? Maybe you'll fall back in love with teaching, or maybe you will simply find new ways to hold onto the passion that you never lost but hope to maintain. This is not about toxic positivity or pretending everything is easy. It is about embracing all of it: the good, the messy, and every complicated, beautiful moment in between.

CHAPTER 10

More Than Showing Up: How Trust Turns Classrooms into Communities

What does it take for a student to truly trust you, and how do you know when they do?

Teaching isn't just about lessons and grades; it's about trust. Every meaningful classroom moment begins with a relationship strong enough to hold both laughter and mistakes. When students know they are seen and valued, learning stops feeling like a checklist and starts feeling like an adventure.

Love

The teachers we remember are not the ones who just handed out information and graded papers. We remember the ones who made us feel seen, the ones who looked at us and somehow knew there was more inside us than we believed. That kind of love builds confidence in students who might otherwise doubt themselves. It offers steady ground to kids who find chaos everywhere else. It builds a classroom where failure is not something to fear but an opportunity for growth. Teaching without love is just standards, paperwork, and test scores. Building meaningful relationships with our students turns it into something real. Yes, hard days are going to happen. Budgets will get slashed, workloads will pile up, and there will be mornings when you wonder why you ever thought you could survive a career fueled by cold coffee, a bladder of steel, and hope. Building relationships with our students won't fix everything, but loving our students turns a long list of names into real stories, real hopes, and real dreams. Loving our students does not mean we should not be fighting for better pay, better support, and less nonsense on our plates. We should, and we must. But love makes the noise a little easier to tune out. It reminds us of where the real work happens, and it keeps our purpose louder than all the things we cannot control.

Unfortunately, teachers seem to be losing the battle in education. If you are an administrator or policymaker, hear this: we need you to start listening to the teachers who are in the trenches every day. We know what students need, and it starts with building meaningful relationships in our classrooms. When we teach with compassion and love, we create ripples of compassion and resilience that stretch far beyond any lesson plan, test score, rubric, or observation. We are growing not just smarter students, but stronger humans, and we cannot keep doing it alone. We need your support.

Start Small and Share

How can I create a space where my students feel safe, happy, and given the potential to thrive, no matter their ability, background, or achievement level? How can I authentically build relationships in my classroom? For me, I start small. As my students come in and find their seats, I give them a couple of minutes to get settled before asking, "Alright, who has something they want to share today?" I always remind them to keep it short and sweet, because everyone deserves a turn, and yes, even I share too. Some of the things my students have shared make me laugh while others remind me why this work is so personal.

If you're still questioning using part of your precious class time for simple chit chat, research backs this up. Oxford Learning points to Christina Hinton's doctoral study, which explored the relationship between happiness, motivation, and academic achievement among elementary and high school students. Hinton found a clear positive connection between student happiness and both motivation and academic performance. Her work also emphasizes the critical role that strong relationships with teachers and peers play in fostering student happiness. The article goes on to support the impact of prioritizing social connections, recognizing the power of happiness by weaving in simple daily practices.[1] It's amazing what you learn during those quick shares like who lost a tooth, who brought a worm to school because it looked lonely, and who named themselves Captain Waffles for the week. Somehow these simple shares begin to turn strangers into a community. Here are a couple of shares, among many, that stand out to me.

A candid third grader with a quick wit: During our usual morning share, one of my third graders raised her hand and said, with total honesty and zero embarrassment, "We lost our soccer game thirteen to zero." I looked at her, knowing she had a good sense of humor, laughed a little, and replied. "Oh wow, they really whopped y'all, but hey, the good news is your team has nowhere to go but up." That weekend, I ran into her and her parents at a local coffee shop. My student was proudly wearing her soccer uniform. I gave her a big smile, fist bump, and said, "Okay, go get 'em this weekend! I hope to hear about a win next week."

Sure enough, Monday rolls around and she walks in with a grin and proudly says, "We only lost six to zero this time." Her classmates cheered. The following week she came in and announced that her team had tied. At this point, the class basically treated it like she had won the World Cup, and then the final week of the season arrived. She came into class with this confident little strut and a shiny medal hanging around her neck. I saved her for last during our share time because I could tell she had something special to share. When I finally called on her, she tried to keep a straight face but couldn't hold back the smile. She told the class that her team had played in a tournament that weekend and won first place. She also shared that she had scored four goals throughout the tournament. The classroom erupted like we'd all won the tournament. I asked her if I could wear

---

[1] "The Power of Happiness and Connection in Education." Oxford Learning, July 2, 2025. https://www.oxfordlearning.com/the-power-of-happiness-and-connection-in-education/.

her medal and take a selfie. She smiled and said, "Only if I get to be in the picture." In that moment, she wasn't just proud of herself, she was inviting me into her victory, and I'll take that any day over accomplishing my forced "data driven goal."

A wide-eyed first grader with boundless enthusiasm: One morning during our share time, a little boy waved his hand in the air with so much enthusiasm that I thought he was about to announce a new puppy. I called on him, and with complete sincerity he said, "My grandpa died this weekend. He burned up in a house fire."

The room went silent. My heart sank. I gently offered my condolences and asked if he wanted to talk to the counselor or maybe take some quiet time in our reading nook. He shrugged and said he was okay. He didn't really know his grandpa that well since he lived far away in another state. What happened next was one of those small but unforgettable moments that makes you believe in the goodness of kids. Throughout the day, I watched his classmates rise to the occasion in their own first-grade way. One offered him a hug. Another quietly placed a stuffed animal on his desk. One student, who normally spent most of the day upside down in his chair, handed him a crayon drawing of an angel floating on a cloud. They didn't need a lesson plan to know what to do. They just showed up for him the way little humans do when we let kindness lead the way.

A first grader whose imagination could outshine any spotlight: This might go down as one of my all-time favorite morning shares. One day, a bold and bubbly girl, we'll call her Ashlynn, raised her hand with the confidence of someone who's about to drop major news. She proceeded to tell the class, "I made it to the next round of America's Got Talent."

"Wait, what? Ashlynn, how am I just now hearing about this? What's your talent? What round are you on? When does it air? Do I need to record it?" I wanted answers.

She smiled and said that she performed an original song she wrote herself. I asked if she'd feel comfortable singing it for the class, and she politely declined. Totally fair. I told her no pressure, but "Please don't forget me when you're famous."

A few days later as I was walking home from school, I ran into her father who works at the nearby high school. Naturally, I greeted him with, "Oh my gosh! I cannot believe what Ashlynn has accomplished!"

He looked puzzled. "What are you talking about, Ms. Chang?"

"Ashlynn!" I said. "She made it to the next round of America's Got Talent. She wrote a song! She performed it! This is huge!"

After an awkward pause he said "Um, I hate to break it to you, Ms. Chang, but Ashlynn has never even auditioned for America's Got Talent. She does love the show though."

I stood there, trying to piece it all together, wondering if I somehow imagined the whole thing. Maybe I mixed up my students? Surely, I was mistaken. The following day, I saw Ashlynn in the hallway and asked her about it. Her eyes widened like she thought she was in trouble. I assured her that I was not angry, but I just wanted to make sure I remembered the story correctly. She looked down and murmured, "I made it up, but I really do want to be on America's Got Talent," and I simply laughed. I could not decide if I was more surprised or secretly proud that she had pulled this off. I gave her a big hug and said, "Ashlynn, I don't know if you'll become a famous singer-songwriter, but you've definitely got a gift for storytelling, and if there's ever a round for creative imagination, you've already won."

A shy fifth grader with quick hands and a quicker mind: A shy young boy who rarely shares during optional share time walked into class one day fidgeting with a Rubik's Cube. He was one of my quieter students. The kind of kid who usually opted out of morning share time and would sit back and listen to others, but one day, as he sat and listened to share after share, he fidgeted with the Rubik's Cube. Naturally, I had questions.

"Wait a minute," I said. "Can you actually solve that thing? I can do one side, but that's all."

He looked up, nodded, and replied confidently. "Yeah, I can solve it in under three minutes."

Now, I don't pass up moments like this. I grinned and asked if he'd be up for a little challenge. Would he feel okay solving it while I timed him in front of the class? He lit up. The quiet kid who usually avoided the spotlight was suddenly ready for center stage. I grabbed my phone, hit the timer, and he got to work. The room went quiet as we all watched in awe, and 2 minutes and 23 seconds later, the cube was solved, and the room went wild. It was one of those moments where you watch a kid come alive in a way you hadn't seen before, and just like that, our quiet friend became the Rubik's Cube legend of the classroom.

Let me be clear, optional share time isn't all sunshine and giggles. If left wide open, it can quickly turn into a competitive game of "who had the most Instagram-worthy weekend." One kid says they saw a movie, which somehow inspires the next kid to say they went to the beach. Then someone casually drops, "My family went to France," followed by another who proudly declares, "That's cool, but I went to the moon." Meanwhile, a quiet student in the back who didn't leave the house all weekend starts to sink into their seat feeling a bit awkward. That's why I'm careful with how I frame it. I don't make it all about weekend recaps. In fact, I encourage students to share other things such as a book they're reading, something they noticed on the way to school, how the weather made them feel, a favorite video game, even a weird dream. I want to give students a voice without making it a competition, because share time isn't about impressing anyone. It's about making connections.

After seeing how open-ended share time can sometimes lead to unintentional comparisons or leave quieter students feeling left out, I knew I needed a better way to get everyone involved. I wanted to give students an opportunity to share without requiring kids to open up about their personal lives if they weren't ready. That's when I started using simple prompts like "This or That" and "Would You Rather." These quick, low-pressure questions give every student a chance to participate and feel seen, without putting anything too personal on the table. It's a small shift, but it makes a big difference especially for the kids who may not want to talk about their weekend.

Here are a few examples to get the conversations flowing:

- Would you rather play a video game or read a book?
- Would you rather win one million dollars in one chunk or have someone give you a penny and double that money every day for one month?

- Would you rather sweat honey or lemonade?
- Would you rather have spaghetti hair or pizza sliced feet?
- Would you rather explore space or the deep ocean?
- Would you rather meet Steph Curry or Taylor Swift?
- Would you rather never have homework or never take tests in school?

The beauty of these prompts is how easy they are to adjust for different age groups. With first graders, I might ask them to choose between pizza and tacos and explain their answer in a full sentence using "because." By third grade, students are writing full paragraphs with two or three reasons while researching and adding an interesting fact they found on the Internet. Teachers can also tweak the questions to match whatever subject they're teaching. Want to connect it to science? Ask if students would rather visit the moon or dive to the bottom of the ocean. Covering social studies? Let them choose between traveling back in time or exploring a new country. "Would You Rather" questions can be lighthearted, curiosity-sparking, and surprisingly effective at building classroom community. They help students feel more at ease, get them talking and laughing, and naturally ease them into the learning mindset without feeling like a warm-up quiz.

After our class has completed our "Would you rather" questions, I dive into one of my favorite traditions: the Joke of the Week. I first got the idea from a fellow teacher who always seemed to have her class giggling before the bell even finished ringing. Later, I told her I'd shamelessly borrowed her idea, as all great teachers do. She laughed and said, "Just a heads-up, an admin asked me why I was telling jokes that had nothing to do with the lesson and actually dinged me on my official teacher observation." I nodded thoughtfully, then immediately decided to keep the joke anyway, because starting the day with a joke does more than just get a few giggles, it sets the tone. It helps students relax, builds classroom community, and signals that our room is a space where joy and learning go hand in hand. A shared laugh can break down walls, spark conversation, and remind students (and teachers) that it's okay to have fun while doing serious work. In fact, I've found that those few silly seconds often make the minutes that follow more focused and productive.

At the end of the day, teaching is not just about standards or strategies, it's about relationships. It's about choosing to see the whole child, not just the one who turns in homework on time or raises their hand the most. It's about loving kids even when they're hard to love and showing up for them not just as their teacher, but as a consistent and caring adult. When we take the time to build real relationships, when we learn their stories, celebrate their quirks, and remind them that they matter, we create something far more powerful than just academic success. We create a sense of belonging, a safe place to land, and a reason to try again.

CHAPTER 11

More Than a Smile: The Power of Joyful Classrooms

When was the last time laughter changed the mood of your classroom, and what made it possible?

There's something magical that happens when laughter fills a classroom. It softens the edges of a tough day, brings students closer together, and reminds everyone, even the teacher, that learning can be both meaningful and fun. Humor in the classroom isn't just about cracking jokes or entertaining students. It's about intentionally creating space for joy, vulnerability, and connection. It's about using laughter to build trust, ease anxiety, and make learning feel a little lighter and a lot more fun. Whether it's a well-placed joke, a silly voice during a read-aloud, or just poking fun at my own mistakes, I've found that humor can break down barriers and create a classroom culture where kids feel seen, safe, and connected. This chapter is about more than making students laugh. It's about using humor as a powerful teaching tool to spark joy, build trust, and make room for the kind of learning that lasts.

Deciding to intentionally use humor in my classroom was never a question, because humor always came naturally for me. As a kid with a disability, humor became my shield. It was how I protected myself, how I took back a little power in moments that felt anything but kind. I will always remember those bus rides home when my peers would play "Who's the Stinky Kid," and the culprit was always me.

They'd point, snicker, and wait for my reaction like it was part of the routine. I learned quickly not to flinch, but instead, I leaned into it with a fake grin and a practiced retort. "Yep, it's me! I win again! What do I win?" At the time, those one-liners felt like little victories, but looking back, I realize they were survival strategies. Cringey? Maybe, but for a disabled kid trying to survive the longest, most painful part of the day, those punchlines were my armor. That experience of being laughed at and finding a way to take control shaped the teacher I am today. I no longer use humor to hide pain. I use it to build a connection. In my classroom, laughter is not a shield; it's a bridge. It helps create a joy for learning while building a community. I've seen how powerful humor can be when it lifts people up instead of tearing them down, and I carry that lesson with me every single day.

Senior Associate Director of Teaching & Learning at UGA Dr. Ruth Poproski explains, "When students laugh, they are more relaxed and more able to engage in learning...it gives them permission to say things that may or may not be right. It lowers the stakes for participation."[1] When students are relaxed and laughing, they let their guard down. They'll start raising their hands without overthinking. They'll participate without feeling judged, and that is when the real learning starts to happen. Humor in the classroom can be a powerful tool, but like any good tool, it works best when used with purpose. It is not about being the class clown or scoring easy laughs for cool points. It is about using humor to engage, to clarify, and to connect the dots in ways that stick. Ted Powers, a professor of psychology at Parkland College in Illinois (2005), suggests that effective teachers should not tell jokes just to be funny. He explains, "Humor in the classroom is most effective when linked to concepts being studied. Humor for the sake of humor might make you a 'cooler' teacher in the eyes of some students, but humor that educates will help you become a more effective instructor for all students."[2] Finding that sweet spot between entertaining and educating students takes careful thought and intention.

---

[1] "Why so Serious? Three Reasons to Use Humor in Your Classroom." On Teaching and Learning @ Georgia Tech, October 22, 2018. https://blog.ctl.gatech.edu/2017/12/15/why-so-serious-three-reasons-to-use-humor-in-your-classroom/.

[2] Powers, Ted. "Engaging Students With Humor." *Observer*, Association for Psychological Science, December 1, 2005. https://www.psychologicalscience.org/observer/engaging-students-with-humor.

It is easy to fall into the trap of simply using humor just to get a laugh, but the real impact comes when that humor truly supports learning. Poproski and Powers may offer different perspectives, but they both land on the same core idea that incorporating humor in the classroom is an effective teaching strategy. When used thoughtfully, humor becomes a powerful teaching tool that both lightens the mood and deepens the learning.

The question remains: how can teachers integrate humor into today's classrooms in a way that is both intentional and appropriate? Remember the "Joke of the Week" I mentioned in the last chapter? As students enter the room, their eyes go straight to the whiteboard where the joke is waiting. Almost instantly, the guessing begins. It becomes a lighthearted routine that builds excitement and sets a positive tone for the day. A quick Internet search will give you hundreds of school-friendly options to choose from. Here are a few examples to get you started:

- Why do teachers wear sunglasses? Because their students are so *bright.*
- Why was the math book sad? Because it had a lot of *problems.*
- Who's the king of the classroom? The *Ruler.*
- What did the ocean say to the shore? Nothing; it *waved.*
- Why did the computer go to the beach? To *surf* the Internet.

As students begin to understand the puns and wordplay, they often come up with responses that are just as clever and often funnier than the original answer itself. In one second-grade class, when I asked, "What did the ocean say to the shore?" a student answered, "How are you? I *shore* hope you're having a great day." In a first-grade class later that year, I asked why a computer might go to the beach, and without missing a beat, students excitedly chimed in with answers like, "To *recharge*," "Because the beach is their *type* of place," and "Because it's the *key* to their happiness." Moments like these are more than just funny, they're signs of creative thinking taking root. What may seem like simple silliness is the spark of something deeper. As their wordplay sharpens and their confidence blooms, I'm reminded that some of the most meaningful growth doesn't fit on a data chart.

Now, I know some of you might be thinking, "Wait a minute! I can't start class with a joke. I don't have time, and if it isn't directly tied to the objective, my administration might dock me during an observation." Trust me, I've likely heard it and experienced it before. Therefore, if you find yourself needing to convince your admin, or anyone else, that humor is an effective teaching tool, you're in good company. Let's take a moment to unpack the science and heart behind that laughter, because there is compelling evidence behind the use of laughter in learning environments.

The Science Behind Laughter

In a CNN interview, cognitive psychologist Janet Gibson highlights the benefits of laughter, explaining that "as you laugh, it lowers your adrenaline levels and, over a longer time frame, your levels of the stress hormone cortisol." She goes on to note that "laughter can improve your mood and make your physical and emotional response to stress less intense. You're more relaxed, less stressed, and you have a pleasant buzzy feeling."[3] Building on this perspective, the Mayo Clinic calls laughter "the best medicine." They offer practical strategies for incorporating more laughter into daily life. According to their findings, laughter stimulates our organs, reduces stress, relieves pain, boosts the immune system, and elevates our mood.[4] These findings extend into the field of education as well. Researchers Segrist and Hupp have compiled a range of studies, resources, and strategies designed to help educators integrate meaningful humor into the classroom. Together, this evidence makes one thing clear: humor and laughter can be a valuable educational tool when used effectively.[5] While there's plenty of research backing the value of humor in education, sometimes what we often need are clear, actionable reasons to try it ourselves.

---

[3] Hunt, Katie. "The Science of Laughter and Why It's Good for Us." *CNN*, July 1, 2021. https://www.cnn.com/2021/07/01/health/science-of-laughter-scn-wellness/index.html.

[4] Mayo Clinic. "Stress Relief from Laughter? It's No Joke," n.d. https://www.mayoclinic.org/healthy-lifestyle/stress-management/in-depth/stress-relief/art-20044456.

[5] Dan J. Segrist and Stephen D. A. Hupp, *This Class Is a Joke! Humor as a Pedagogical Tool in the Teaching of Psychology* (Edwardsville, IL: Southern Illinois University Edwardsville, 2015).

Using humor in your classroom can:

1. **Build Rapport:** Humor reduces tension and makes the classroom feel safe, thus encouraging students to relax and participate more openly. As a result of feeling safe and relaxed, students are more likely to trust and relate to their teachers. A well-timed joke or lighthearted moment helps bridge the gap between teacher and student, fostering a sense of equality and mutual understanding. When teachers use humor, they appear more approachable and relatable, making it easier for students to connect on a personal level.

   When students laugh with their teacher, it strengthens the bond between them, creating a sense of camaraderie that feels more like teamwork rather than the usual dynamic of authority and obedience. It's as if everyone in the room is saying, "We're in this together." A teacher who knows when to laugh often understands their students on a deeper level, and that understanding tells students, "I see you. I get you." More than anything, humor has the power to transform the classroom into a community. It fosters a sense of shared joy where students feel like they belong and can trust their teacher. It's not just about making lessons fun. It's about making the classroom a place where everyone wants to be.

2. **Improve Student Behavior:** One of the most common complaints I hear from teachers is how to deal with "kids these days." I hear numerous accounts of teachers craving respect from their students and asking administrators and parents for additional support. Using humor in our classrooms helps students relax and feel less anxious. When students share a laugh, they're more likely to work well together and less likely to act out. Plus, a good joke can ease any tension and shift everyone's energy in a positive direction and stop problems before they even start. A fun and positive atmosphere makes students look forward to class. When students associate the classroom with joy and lightheartedness, they're more likely to bring a positive attitude and good behavior into the space. Humor is an excellent tool for keeping students' attention and engaged, thus setting up a space for success.

Although I wholeheartedly believe in the correlation between humor and student behavior, I want to make something abundantly clear. I am not suggesting that using humor in your classroom will fix all student behaviors. I am, however, proposing that if used correctly and intentionally, using humor in class has a positive impact on student behaviors. Humor makes the classroom feel safe and welcoming, where students are less afraid of being wrong or judged which leads to increased engagement and better behavior.

3. **Reduce Stress:** According to Natalie Dattilo, instructor of psychology at Harvard University, "Nobody knows precisely why we laugh…We do know something about what it does, though. Psychologically, it improves mood almost immediately and lowers stress and anxiety. Physically, it lowers levels of cortisol, the stress hormone, while raising the "feel good" neurotransmitters dopamine and serotonin.[6] However, does using humor in the classroom lower stress among our students? According to research, laughter has many benefits.[7] I'm not saying that teachers should be constantly laughing and never take things seriously; however, making learning fun can be a powerful tool to academic success.

4. **Allow for Mistakes:** Using humor in the classroom creates a more relaxed and supportive environment, which helps students feel less afraid of making mistakes. When teachers respond to errors with a sense of humor, it lightens the mood and shows students that mistakes are a natural part of learning and not something to be ashamed of. It's important to note that responding with humor should never involve embarrassing the student for their mistake. Instead, shift the focus away from the student and use humor to lighten the mood, perhaps by making yourself the subject of the joke.

---

[6] Powell, Alvin, and Alvin Powell. "A Laugh a Day Keeps the Doctor Away?" Harvard Gazette, January 10, 2024. https://news.harvard.edu/gazette/story/2023/01/a-laugh-a-day-keeps-the-doctor-away/.

[7] Scott, Elizabeth. "The Health Benefits of Laughter." Verywell Mind, May 8, 2024. https://www.verywellmind.com/the-stress-management-and-health-benefits-of-laughter-314508.

For example, you could say, "This problem stumped me too, and I actually get paid to teach it!" This approach keeps the tone light and helps students feel comfortable rather than singled out. Humor helps to take the pressure off, encouraging students to take risks, try new things, and learn from their errors without fear of judgment. It fosters a culture where students feel comfortable making mistakes and see them as opportunities to grow.

5. **Enhance Memory:** Using humor in the classroom can significantly enhance students' memory by making the learning experience more engaging and memorable. When students find something funny, their brains are more likely to pay attention and retain the information. Humor grabs attention and creates emotional connections with the material, which strengthens memory retention. According to Sarah Henderson, a high school English teacher and graduate of Johns Hopkins University, "Humor activates the brain's dopamine reward system, stimulating goal-oriented motivation and long-term memory, which means that humor can improve retention in students of all ages."[8] Humor helps students process information in a more relaxed and enjoyable environment, thus reducing stress and allowing for better focus. Additionally, humor often creates vivid mental associations, making it easier for students to recall key concepts later. By incorporating humor into lessons, teachers can make learning more enjoyable and increase the likelihood that students will remember what they've learned.

6. **Encourage Creative Thinking:** As an elementary gifted education teacher, I believe that schools place too much emphasis on achievement and performance data rather than creative thinking (I'll dive more into this a bit later), but according to Forbes, 70% of employers "say creative

---

[8] Henderson, Sarah. "Laughter and Learning: Humor Boosts Retention." Edutopia, March 31, 2015. https://www.edutopia.org/blog/laughter-learning-humor-boosts-retention-sarah-henderson.

thinking is (was) the most in-demand skill in 2024."[9] Using humor requires the ability to combine ideas in novel ways and challenges traditional patterns of thinking. It encourages flexibility in how we approach problems or situations. For example, a joke might rely on wordplay, irony, or exaggeration, which requires thinking creatively to identify links between ideas. Additionally, humor can help one break through mental blocks, thus allowing for innovative thinking and problem-solving.

7. **Develop Intelligence and Abstract Thinking:** Humor isn't just about making people laugh; it's a clever mental workout that taps into a whole range of intellectual skills. Take cognitive flexibility, for example. To craft a joke, you often see the perspective from a different angle. The more you understand how words can bend and stretch, the sharper your brain becomes at handling complex ideas. Humor requires problem-solving. You know those jokes that make you go "Wait, what?" when you first hear them? They take something that doesn't quite fit and make it work in a surprising or clever way.

   Humor also thrives on emotional intelligence, too. It's knowing when to drop the punchline, how to read the room, and what will make everyone laugh without crossing any lines. When expanding on Gardner's Theory of Multiple Intelligences, Cherry explains that people with linguistic-verbal intelligence "use humor when telling stories."[10]

   Finally, humor invites you to think abstractly. The best jokes take seemingly unrelated ideas and turn them into something clever, stretching your brain to make connections you wouldn't normally see. It's like a puzzle, where the pieces might not seem to fit, but when they do, it's a moment of pure creative brilliance. Lecturer Lowri Dowthwaite-Walsh of

---

[9] Wells, Rachel. "70% of Employers Say Creative Thinking Is Most In-Demand Skill in 2024." *Forbes*, January 28, 2024. https://www.forbes.com/sites/rachelwells/2024/01/28/70-of-employers-say-creative-thinking-is-most-in-demand-skill-in-2024/.

[10] Cherry, Kendra. "Gardner's Theory of Multiple Intelligences." Verywell Mind, January 29, 2025. https://www.verywellmind.com/gardners-theory-of-multiple-intelligences-2795161.

the University of Central Lancashire points to research from Austria showing that people with a strong sense of humor tend to have higher IQs than those who don't.[11] While not every student needs to be a stand-up comic, this study reinforces the idea that humor can signal intellectual depth. So, the next time someone questions your use of humor in the classroom, point to the research and remind them that humor and intelligence often go hand in hand.

The benefits of teachers using humor in the classroom are well-documented and compelling. Not only does humor enhance student engagement and learning, but it also creates a positive and enjoyable environment. These reasons alone should encourage educators to incorporate humor into their teaching practices. When teachers laugh with their students, it fosters a sense of connection while also reducing stress and releasing endorphins, which can make teaching more enjoyable. In a profession where educators often have little control over school policies or external demands, one thing remains within our power: how we choose to deliver our content and interact with our students.

Ed Dunkelblau, former president of the Association for Applied and Therapeutic Humor and Director of the Institute for Emotionally Intelligent Learning, shared his insights in an interview on humor in education. As a consultant specializing in character education and social-emotional learning (SEL), Dunkelblau stated, "In the present environment of high stakes testing, budgetary challenges, increased demands on educators and competition for students' attention, everyone in the school benefits when humor is part of the pedagogy. Humor builds a learning relationship through the joyful confluence of head and heart." He points to a growing literature on how humor reduces stress and tension in the classroom, improves retention of information, and promotes creative understanding.[12] Research backed evidence highlights the many benefits in our classrooms.

---

[11] Dowthwaite-Walsh, Lowri. "Funny People Are More Intelligent than Their Po-Faced Peers." *The Conversation*, October 16, 2017. https://theconversation.com/funny-people-are-more-intelligent-than-their-po-faced-peers-84709.
[12] Elias, Maurice J. "Using Humor in the Classroom." Edutopia, March 30, 2015. https://www.edutopia.org/blog/using-humor-in-the-classroom-maurice-elias?page=1%2C1.

Lujan and DiCarlo acknowledge that humor and laughter may not directly cause learning, but they emphasize that humor creates conditions conducive to learning. And while a teacher's primary focus should always be on student learning, making the process enjoyable can have a profound and lasting impact.[13]

It's not uncommon for teachers to be remembered by former students, but what they recall might surprise you. For me, former students often share experiences that center around my sense of humor and how I made learning fun rather than a learning objective, lesson plan, or even a really cool PBL project that I spent months creating. This realization hits even closer to home when I think about my youngest son, who frequently describes school as "the worst place ever." I felt the same way when I was his age, and I can't help but wonder, what if more classrooms embraced humor as part of his learning experience? What if students looked forward to school because it was fun and not just academic? I believe we might see not only improved behavior but also a rise in engagement and academic success.

---

[13] Lujan, Heidi L., and Stephen E. DiCarlo. "Humor Promotes Learning!" *AJP Advances in Physiology Education* 40, no. 4 (October 4, 2016): 433–34. https://doi.org/10.1152/advan.00123.2016.

CHAPTER 12

Oops, Now What? When Humor Goes Too Far

How do you know the difference between using humor to build a bridge versus creating a barrier?

I'm a huge believer in using humor in the classroom, but let's be clear, not all humor is created equal. When used well, humor can build trust, spark engagement, and create a classroom culture where students feel safe to take risks while having a little fun. However, when it's misused, it can do the opposite like alienate, embarrass, or even harm. That's why I believe humor in the classroom should come with careful consideration.

Now, this is usually where the middle and high school teachers jump in and say, "Hold on! Wait a minute! Using sarcasm and roasting is how we survive teenagers!" Trust me! I understand where that's coming from. Although I currently teach elementary school, I have had my fair share of working with both middle and high school students. I taught high school ESOL in a large Metro Atlanta school, where many of my students had recently immigrated to the U.S. Some came with their families in search of a better life. Others had been sent alone, living with distant relatives, juggling school and work while carrying hopes for opportunities bigger than themselves. These weren't kids who needed to be "roasted." They needed to feel seen, respected, and yes, they needed to laugh, but they needed a laughter that lifted them up, not alienated them.

Humor can be an excellent tool in the classroom, but it can also have unintended consequences. For example, one poorly timed joke can alienate students or create an awkward environment for some. Jokes that touch on sensitive topics such as stereotypes may single out students, thus leading to embarrassment or resentment like when my high school health teacher made fun of gay people by making a joke about God creating Adam and Eve and not Adam and Steve. I can assure that although not stated directly to me, his "joke" left me feeling isolated and unwelcome in his class. Even light-hearted teasing that seems well received can damage the trust between a teacher and their students. This trust is essential for effective teaching, and repairing it can be difficult once broken. Using sarcasm or super subtle humor can be a bit tricky. What one student finds hilarious might leave another feeling left out or withdrawn. Teachers should keep in mind that their classrooms are full of students with all kinds of experiences and perspectives, so make sure your jokes bring everyone together and so not leave anyone feeling excluded. Finally, it's important to recognize that not all students respond to humor in the same way. While some may find jokes engaging, others may feel excluded if they don't "get" the humor. We should strive to maintain a balanced and thoughtful approach when incorporating humor into our classrooms. However, what happens when teachers mess up and make that sarcastic joke, the one at the expense of the student, or implement practices that are harmful to students?

When I began writing this book, I found myself reminiscing about all the things I had done right throughout my career. I wanted to inspire teachers to be the best they can be, but the truth is, I am far from perfect. I make mistakes. I even look back at some of my past teaching practices and cringe a little. Things I thought were effective at the time completely miss the mark today. For example, when I first started teaching, I was advised to use a clip system to track student behaviors. My clip system mimicked a redlight. I would write each child's name on a clothes pin and throughout the day if a student exhibited a behavior that I deemed unworthy, I would move their clip from green to yellow and possibly red. At the end of the day, I would write the child's clip color in an agenda for parents/ guardians to sign and return the following day, but here's the thing, I do better now. I will continue to improve, no matter how long

I have been teaching. It's about showing up and getting a little better every day.

For those of you saying that using a behavior chart system is easy and effective, I want to and assure you that publicly displaying students' behaviors for all to see is, in fact, not an effective classroom management strategy. Throughout the years, educational professionals have advised against using clip charts or points systems in our classrooms. Although it may be a simple way to monitor student behaviors, Blankman explains, "Public shaming is public shaming, no matter how colorful and bright you make it."[1] If we're managing students by putting them on blast for every little mistake, we're basically shutting the door on creating a space where students feel safe to be themselves. If we want students to take risks, learn from their mistakes, and show a little vulnerability, we need to make psychological safety a top priority.

Looking back, I realize that this public shaming and flippant behavior system failed my students and did nothing to elicit the behaviors I desired among my students. As easy as it is to portray myself as Teacher of the Year material, I also come with mistakes. However, it's the mistakes that give us an opportunity to learn, grow, and even serve as a role model for our students. Without further ado, please proceed to read this story as a learning opportunity, and as a teacher who loves using humor in my classroom even when I miss the mark.

Many years ago, I taught general education, first grade, and I had a kid named Michael. Michael was identified as highly gifted, and he was incredibly curious, always asking questions that seemed wise beyond his years. He had a knack for picking up concepts quickly, often surprising adults with his deep understanding or quirky connections between ideas. However, when things didn't click right away, his enthusiasm could quickly turn into frustration. He might cross his arms and say something like, "I can't do this! This is impossible!" Michael had a strong desire to get things just right and without complication, so when I encouraged Michael to complete a task independently, he was not having it.

---

[1] ASCD. "Your Clip Chart Is Ruining Your Classroom Culture," November 29, 2023. https://ascd.org/blogs/your-clip-chart-is-ruining-your-classroom-culture.

Many of you are likely familiar with the classic first-grade science activity exploring how plants grow, thus giving kids a front-row seat to the plant life cycle. Each child gets a dry lima bean, a small handful of cotton balls, a Ziploc bag, and some water. The teacher explains how plants need water, sunlight, and air to grow. The kids soak their cotton balls in water (squeezing out the extra so they're damp, not dripping), then wrap them snugly around the lima bean. Next, they gently place the cotton-wrapped bean inside the Ziploc bag and seal it shut. Then the teacher helps them tape their bags to a sunny window, so the bean gets plenty of light. Everyone writes their name on their bag to keep track of whose bean is whose. Over the next few days, the students excitedly watch as their beans sprout. First, they might spot tiny roots poking out, followed by the shoot reaching upward. The transparent bag makes it easy to see the progress without disturbing the bean. Each day, students, dressed in lab coats and goggles, record their observations in a science journal, drawing pictures and writing about what they see each day, and there's always that one bean that refuses to sprout so you grow a secret bean at home and switch it out one day without the children knowing. It's a simple activity, but it's packed with big lessons: how plants grow, why sunlight and water matter, and how even a small seed can turn into something incredible with just a little patience and care.

The room was filled with excitement as the budding scientists taped their bags onto the window. Michael walked over to me and said, "Ms. Chang, I can't get my cotton ball around my bean, will you do it for me?" To which I replied, "Michael, if I give you a fish, I have merely fed you for a day; however, if I teach you how to fish, I will feed you for life." Of course, Michael understood absolutely nothing about this proverbial piece of wisdom, because he was six years old. However, what he heard me say was "No Michael I am not going to help you. Do it yourself." Michael began to spiral. "You never help me!" he snapped, tears welling up in his eyes. "I can't do it, and it's not fair. You are a terrible teacher. I don't like you."

I encouraged him to try again. He tried again, wrapping the cotton ball too tightly this time, causing it to rip, and that was the last straw. Michael let out a loud wail, throwing the bean onto the floor and collapsing onto the chair with his arms crossed. "I'm not doing it anymore! It's stupid!" This is when I decided to use a strategy that often works well for me: humor. I felt that if I said something funny, I could diffuse the situation and help assuage Michael's frustrations, so without missing a beat, I said something along the lines of "Michael, c'mon you got this. Why are you being such a butt about a silly little bean," and just as I expected, Michael busted out with laughter as I called him a butt.

"Wait, you can't say that. You're the teacher," a girl said from the other side of the room. Just as I was about to clapback with another joke, I realized she was right. "You know what? You're right," I said. "I shouldn't have said that. I owe all of you and especially Michael an apology. I made a joke and called Michael a 'butt.' I thought it was funny at the time, but I realize now that I may have hurt Michael's feelings. That was not my intention, and I'm really sorry, Michael. I want everyone to know that it's important to be kind and respectful to each other. Sometimes, jokes can make others feel bad, and I will do my best to be more careful with my words from now on."

As soon as I got the class back on task, I asked Michael to come up to my desk so I could give him my ACE apology.

The ACE Three-Part Apology Strategy (*J. Chang, 2025*)

The ACE Apology Strategy (Acknowledge, Commit, Execute) is designed to help individuals take responsibility for their actions in a clear, effective, and professional manner. This approach fosters trust, accountability, and continuous improvement. Here's how it works:

A (Acknowledge): The first step is to honestly ***acknowledge*** that you made a mistake. This means recognizing what you did, how it might have affected the student or others, and offer a sincere apology. It's not just about saying "I'm sorry," it's about showing that you understand the impact of your actions. When you acknowledge the mistake openly, you show students that you care about their feelings, take responsibility, and are committed to making things right. This helps rebuild trust and creates an opportunity for healing and moving forward.

C (Commit): After acknowledging your mistake, the next step is to ***commit*** to doing better moving forward. This means more than just saying, "I won't do it again." It means making a real and thoughtful effort to change your behavior and take steps to prevent the same mistake from happening again. When students see you actively working to improve, it shows them you're serious about learning and growing. It's about being accountable and showing that you're not just sorry, you're committed to making change.

E (Execute): Finally, it's time to **execute** the apology. This is where you put your commitment into action. It's not enough to say you'll do better. You need to show exactly how. That means explaining the specific steps you'll take to make sure the mistake doesn't happen again. When you share a clear plan and follow through with it, you show others that you're serious about growing and making real change. It builds trust and lets students (and colleagues) know that you're holding yourself accountable in a meaningful way.

For example, I explained to Michael that as his teacher, part of my job is helping him manage big emotions and work through tough moments. I told him that I'm trained to support students during challenges, and if there's ever a time I can't do that effectively, I'll make sure to reach out for help, whether that's from a counselor, an administrator, or even his family. My goal is to make sure that every student, Michael included, gets the care and support they need. Being honest and clear in that moment not only addresses the issue right away, but it also helps build trust between Michael and me. Full transparency showed Michael that I was taking the situation seriously and taking real steps to make it right.

My apology didn't stop there. As soon as I had a break, I picked up the phone and called Michael's home. His mom answered: "Hey Ms. Chang… what did he do this time?" I chuckled and explained the whole story. She burst out laughing and said, "Look, it's OK. He is a butt. I live with him," and just like that, I gave Michael's mom my full ACE apology: Acknowledge, Commit, Execute. She genuinely appreciated the call, accepted my apology, and we wrapped up the conversation on a good note.

Now, imagine how differently that might have gone if I hadn't taken the time to call home. Picture Michael at the end of the day, dragging his oversized backpack, climbing into the car, fumbling with the seatbelt in the carpool lane chaos.

"How was your day, Michael?"

"It was OK… but Ms. Chang called me a butt."

Something tells me that story would've ended very differently.

That's why I always tell teachers: don't underestimate the power of a quick phone call. I get it. I hate making phone calls too. I'd much rather send a ten-page text message or email, but a phone call gives parents a chance to hear your voice, your sincerity, and your good intentions. It's personal, and it builds trust in a way that written words sometimes can't.

Taking time to reflect on my experience with Michael gave me a chance to learn and grow. I don't always get it right the first time, but teaching isn't about perfection; it's about presence. It's about humility. It's about the willingness to pause, reflect, and own our mistakes. Yes, we're going to mess up. We're human, but what matters most is what we do next. Whether the misstep is big or small, we owe it to our students to apologize, to grow, and to do better moving forward. In this profession, our words, our choices, and our responses can leave lasting marks, and sometimes these marks reach far beyond what we ever realize.

CHAPTER 13

The Courage to Ask for Help

Can a teacher pour from an empty cup and still expect students to thrive?

Teachers are expected to be the experts. We're the ones with all the answers, the quick solutions, and the ability to reach every student, but the reality behind the classroom door is often far more complicated. Many teachers struggle quietly and feel the pressure to be everything to everyone. There's often an unspoken rule in many schools: figure it out alone, don't ask for help, and don't admit when you're feeling overwhelmed.

Looking back at the many years I have spent in the classroom, I realize that asking for help is not only a strength; it's essential for teacher survival. We encourage our students to raise their hands when they're confused and ask for help. However, educators should embrace this same mindset. Effective teachers seek out collaboration and support. As Education Editor and Journalist Stephen Noonoo observes, teachers are great at jumping in to help our students, but when it comes to asking for help ourselves, it's a different story. A lot of us avoid reaching out to coworkers for the same reasons kids stay quiet in class. It feels like admitting we don't know what we're doing. Some of us are worried about looking inexperienced or being judged, while others just have no idea what support is even available. Often for newer teachers, there's pressure to always seem upbeat and capable, like they don't want to be a burden.[1]

Teaching was never meant to be a solo act. None of us can do this work in isolation, and the schools that thrive are the ones where asking for help is seen as strength, not weakness.

1. **It promotes professional growth.**

    When teachers seek help from colleagues or mentors, they gain new strategies for instruction, classroom management, and student engagement. Even veteran teachers can find fresh ideas that reinvigorate their practice and lead to continued improvement.

2. **It builds collaboration and community.**

    In a supportive environment, teachers share resources, exchange ideas, and divide responsibilities. Collaboration reduces feelings of isolation and reminds educators they're part of a team working toward a shared purpose.

3. **It reduces stress and increases emotional well-being.**

    Sometimes, help isn't about fixing a problem, it's about being heard. Having a trusted colleague who understands the pressures of teaching can make all the difference. Conversations that validate our experiences help teachers feel seen, supported, and less alone.

4. **It models healthy behavior for students.**

    When leaders and teachers openly seek help, they normalize vulnerability and lifelong learning. Students learn that asking questions and relying on others are signs of strength, not weakness.

So, what happens when you need help, but you don't know where to start, or even realize you need it? What if you work in an unsupportive school? To better illustrate how to ask for help, I will use student behavior as an example. Let's say you're having trouble

---

[1] Stephen, A Noonoo. "How New Teachers Can Learn to Ask for Help." Edutopia, January 27, 2023. https://www.edutopia.org/article/how-new-teachers-can-learn-to-ask-for-help/.

with a particular student, and it's so bad that you can't effectively teach. You've tried everything, but nothing is working. What do you do? Who can you ask for help? For many, we turn to administration, and I can attest that having a supportive admin team can make all the difference. Allow me to share two different scenarios from my personal teaching experience.

Scenario 1: Numbers & Rainbows: During my very first year teaching kindergarten I was a bit nervous, but I walked into my first classroom full of hope and excitement. I wanted to be the kind of teacher who lit a spark in kids, who created a space where learning felt magical, but underneath that enthusiasm was a quiet pressure I had put on myself, and I hoped to prove I could do it. I thought being a "good" teacher meant having picture-perfect lesson plans, smooth transitions, and students who were always on task.

One afternoon, during a math lesson, I noticed one of my students, Lily, leaning over her desk, completely absorbed in something that was completely unrelated to the lesson. I walked over and saw a beautiful drawing of a rainbow in progress. Bright arcs of color spilled across the page, and each stripe perfectly shaded with the kind of care only a child can give. I gently picked it up, and said, "Sweetheart, I love your rainbow, but right now, we need to focus on math. You can finish this later, okay?" I smiled, carefully placed her drawing in her take-home folder so it wouldn't get smudged, and moved on with the lesson, thinking I had handled it with care.

The next morning, I found out that the rainbow had definitely made it home, and it had sparked a storm. Lily's mom marched into my classroom demanding a meeting with the principal. The tone wasn't curious or collaborative, it was furious. Within a few days, we were sitting across from one another in the principal's office, and I could feel the heat radiating off her words. "You stifled her creativity," she said. "You took a rainbow from a six-year-old." I tried to explain that Lily had been struggling in math, that I was only trying to help her stay focused so she wouldn't fall further behind, but before I could finish, my principal gently stepped in.

"She's in her first year of teaching kindergarten," she said, looking at the mother with a calm I hadn't yet learned to carry. "She's still learning, and she cares deeply about your daughter."

The mom didn't miss a beat. "Yes," she said sharply. "That much is clear. She obviously doesn't have much experience with young children."

Oof. That one stung, but I remained professional, sat quietly, and listened. I offered a sincere apology and promised that I would do better, not just for Lily, but for every child who needed to be seen not just as a student, but as a whole human being. I assured her that I would make room for both focus and creativity. For numbers *and* rainbows.

What I thought was a small moment of classroom redirection quickly became something I'll never forget, but not for the reasons I expected. I had genuinely believed I was doing the right thing by helping a student stay focused during math time while still protecting her drawing and treating it kindly. However, when her mother sat across from me, visibly upset, I suddenly found myself on the defensive. I was nervous, caught off guard, and trying to explain my heart. Just as I was finding my voice, my principal spoke over me, not in defense, but in dismissal, shrinking my intentions down to a single label: "first-year kindergarten teacher."

In that moment, I felt small, embarrassed, and unsupported. It didn't feel like someone had my back. It felt like someone had stepped in front of me. As the parent nodded and commented that I clearly didn't have much experience with young children, I sat there, holding back tears, unsure whether to speak or stay silent. I apologized, of course. I promised to do better, but deep down, I wished someone had taken a moment to believe in my intentions, not just excuse my inexperience.

Later, when the meeting ended and the classroom door was closed, I thought hard about what had happened. I realized kids don't split their world into neat little blocks labeled "math" or "art." To them, a rainbow during math makes perfect sense. Learning and joy go hand in hand, and just because I wasn't handing out glitter glue didn't mean I couldn't make space for imagination, but I also realized something else: teachers need space to grow, too. We need grace, encouragement, and support especially in those first years when we're pouring our hearts into the work, terrified of getting it wrong. I didn't need someone to make excuses for me. I needed someone to stand beside me.

That year taught me more than just how to balance expectations with empathy. It taught me that while we're shaping our students, we're also being shaped by our mistakes, our intentions, and the people who choose to lift us up instead of brushing us off, and sometimes the lesson isn't about how to manage a classroom, it's about how to navigate the hard moments when no one steps in to catch you. Yes, kids may need someone to believe in their rainbows, but teachers need someone to believe in them too.

Scenario 2: The Letter: During my twentieth year of teaching, one of my gifted education students, Ian, was having a hard time staying on task. It wasn't anything major; just lots of chatting with his tablemates during instruction and independent work time. After several reminders, I finally did what no student enjoys: I moved his seat.

When I walked the class back to their homeroom for lunch, I asked his teacher if Ian had been showing similar behaviors in her class. Sometimes a second teacher's perspective can offer insight into what's really going on. She confirmed that yes, Ian had frequently been off-task and a bit disruptive with her as well. Later that day, during recess, she had Ian stay back for five to ten minutes to write me an apology letter. I'm not usually a fan of forced apologies or taking away recess, but I appreciated her effort to support me.

After recess, I headed to the third-grade hallway to pick up my students. As we walked back to class, Ian handed me the letter. The front was an apology. He explained that he was sorry for continuously disrupting class and promised it wouldn't happen again, but then I flipped the paper over. On the back, in bold handwriting, Ian had written: *Ms. Chang, you ruined my day. Watch out! I'm about to do the same to you!*

I was not exactly sure what to do, so I reached out for support. I snapped a photo and sent it to my administrator, Ms. Spence. Later that day, the three of us sat in her office while Ms. Spence called Ian's mom. She explained the situation, but Ian's mother immediately jumped in to defend him. "Well, Ms. Chang is just too strict," she said. Without missing a beat, Ms. Spence replied, "Actually, Ms. Chang is probably one of our least strict teachers, and even if she were strict, that doesn't excuse Ian's behavior. He wrote a threatening letter to a teacher. As a result, he will spend a day in in-school suspension and meet with our counselor to ensure that he understands the impact of his words." Ian's mom listened as Ms. Spence explained that Ian would benefit most if we all worked together to support him.

Ian's behavior began to shift within just a couple of weeks. I kept checking in with him, followed the counselor's advice, and made sure to loop in his mom with updates. About a month later, Ian started handing me drawings he'd made at home and telling me that I was his favorite teacher. The same kid who once threatened to ruin my day now made it better.

As many of us know, things don't always turn out that way, but even if Ian's mom hadn't come around, or if his behavior hadn't improved, it still meant the world to know that Ms. Spence had my back and took my concerns seriously.

And honestly? That kind of support hits differently when you've gone through situations where you didn't have it. I've sat in meetings where I felt like I had to prove I wasn't overreacting. I've been talked over, undermined, and left to clean up messes alone, all while trying to smile and stay professional. I've been the teacher who walked away from a parent conference feeling small and unsupported, replaying everything I could've said differently, but not this time.

This time, I felt seen. I felt valued. I felt like the experienced, thoughtful educator I am. Ms. Spence didn't ask me to sugarcoat what had happened or question whether I had handled things "just right." She trusted me. She respected me, and instead of expecting me to handle it all alone, she called the parent, led the conversation with clarity and calm, and made it clear that our school stands behind its teachers, not because we're perfect, but because we're professionals. There's something deeply affirming about that kind of leadership. It doesn't erase the hard parts of teaching, but it makes them bearable. It makes you braver. It reminds you that even when the job feels personal, it's not yours to carry alone.

I walked away from that day not just grateful but energized. When school leaders advocate for teachers and when they speak truth with kindness, show up in the hard conversations, and remind the world that educators deserve respect, it ripples outward. It strengthens school culture. It improves outcomes for kids. It builds a foundation of trust that lets teachers show up, even on the hard days, because at the end of the day, what every teacher wants isn't perfection. It's partnership, and there's no better feeling than knowing your admin not only has your back but believes you're worth backing in the first place.

However, what if you don't have a supportive administrator like Ms. Spence, or if your school lacks access to resources like a counselor? Creating a culture of support isn't just about asking for help, it's also about knowing *how* to ask. When a student's behavior challenges you, approaching the conversation with clarity and purpose can make all the difference.

1. **Be specific.**

   Avoid vague generalizations like "this child is bad" or "they're always misbehaving." Instead, clearly describe the exact behaviors you're seeing and the patterns you've noticed.

2. **Document incidents and strategies.**

   Keep brief notes on what's happening and what you've already tried. This shows initiative and helps administrators see the full picture.

3. **Come prepared with ideas.**

   When you meet with Administration, bring possible solutions. Propose a quick brainstorming session, and show that you're focused on collaboration, not just venting frustration.

4. **Connect your concerns to the bigger picture.**

   Explain how addressing one student's behavior can benefit the entire class by boosting learning, restoring peace, strengthening school culture, and even improving academic outcomes.

5. **Stay persistent and proactive.**

   If the initial conversation stalls, don't give up. Request a follow-up, a professional development session, or even a classroom observation so others can see what you're navigating firsthand.

Yes, we're teachers, but we're also humans and we don't have all the answers. Asking for help shouldn't be seen as a weakness. It should be seen for what it truly is: a commitment to doing what's best for our students. And sometimes the challenges we face feel like way too much for one person to handle. It's not about waving a white flag; it's about showing you care enough to make things better for your students (and yourself). When you team up with your admin, communicate what you need and work together; you're not just solving problems, you're setting the tone for a school culture that thrives on collaboration. So, don't hesitate to speak up, because no one should feel like they're in this alone. When you ask for help, you're building the kind of school community where everyone can thrive.

CHAPTER 14

Recharge, Rethink, Reignite: Smarter PD for the Tired Teacher

When was the last time a professional development left you inspired, and what did that look like?

Teaching can sometimes feel like an endless treadmill. You're constantly moving, constantly doing, and somehow still falling behind. The lesson plans, the ungraded papers, the emails, data, and meetings that could have been emails. It's enough to make even the most passionate educator wonder how they'll keep going, but you don't have to run yourself into the ground to be a great teacher. In fact, some of the best educators I know have mastered the art of working smarter, not harder.

That realization didn't come overnight. Early in my career, I thought being the last car in the parking lot meant I was doing it right. I wore my exhaustion like a badge of honor. I saw burnout as proof that I was committed, but after too many late nights and not enough laughter, I knew something had to give. That's when I started searching for strategies that would make me a more effective teacher without losing myself in the process. One of the most impactful shifts I made was changing how I approached professional development. I stopped seeing it as just another box to check and started treating it like a way to energize a passion I have for teaching. Whether it was a workshop on time management, a podcast about classroom culture, or a national conference that reignited my passion, the right kind of learning gave me what I didn't know I was missing. This job can be demanding, but fresh perspectives and renewed energy help us see that it doesn't have to drain us.

I'll never forget the moment I attended my first National Association for Gifted Children (NAGC) conference. I was teetering on the edge of burnout, so close to walking away from the profession yet again. I wondered if the passion I once felt for teaching was gone for good, but then I walked into that hotel ballroom, and something changed. It wasn't just a conference; it was like a homecoming. I had found my people. Educators lit up talking about asynchronous development and got visibly excited about strategies for supporting twice-exceptional learners. These were professionals who didn't blink when I said *neurodivergent*; they leaned in, and for the first time in a long time, I didn't feel the need to justify or explain why I do what I do. I didn't feel like the odd one out. I felt seen.

At the time, I had felt invisible at my school. I felt like my work wasn't being noticed. I was pouring my energy into lesson plans, advocacy, and student growth, but at my school, it often felt like I was operating in the background. No one asked about the projects I stayed late to finish. No one seemed to notice the extra mile I went for my gifted learners. I wasn't looking for a trophy. I just wanted to feel like I mattered and belonged. That's why the conference hit so hard. It wasn't just the learning. It was the validation. It reminded me that I had something valuable to contribute, and that there were brilliant, passionate, and like-minded people who saw me not as "just" a teacher, but as a professional worth listening to. It gave me back a sense of self I hadn't realized I'd been missing.

That conference reminded me that I wasn't alone in this work. It rekindled the spark that brought me into gifted education in the first place. In gifted education I advocate for gifted learners. And beyond meeting academic needs, I'm honoring identities, amplifying voices, and helping students thrive in a world that often misunderstands them. I walked in feeling invisible, and I walked out energized with fresh ideas, renewed purpose, and the reminder that this job is hard, but it doesn't have to hurt when you're surrounded by people who understand why it matters.

Every session felt like a mini awakening. It was like someone had reached in and gently shaken the part of me that had gone quiet under the weight of burnout. I was snapping photos of slides, bookmarking apps, and taking notes. On the flight home, I opened my laptop and rewrote my entire Monday lesson plan, and not because I had to, but because for the first time in a long time, I wanted to. I was excited. I was hopeful. I remembered what it felt like to love this job with my whole heart.

If you're feeling tired, uninspired, or on the edge of burnout, don't wait for a magic solution to land in your lap. Seek out the people, the spaces, and the moments that remind you who you are and why this work still matters. Professional development isn't just about learning new strategies. It's about reconnecting with your purpose. It's about giving yourself permission to evolve, to ask for help, to laugh, to try something new. You don't have to do it all, and you don't have to do it alone. Just take one small step toward something that lights you up, because when you invest in your own growth from a place of passion, you don't just reignite your teaching, you reignite you.

Not every teacher has access to travel funds, stipends, or even a sub for coverage, but you don't have to leave your zip code or spend a dime to reignite your spark. Professional development comes in many forms, and some of the best growth happens in the spaces we create for ourselves.

Start small and start local. Here are some ideas:

- Look for district offerings that speak to your passions.
- Find an afterschool webinar or a podcast you can listen to on the drive home.
- Follow educators on social media who challenge and inspire you.
- Create a text thread with teachers from other schools.
- Start a book study with someone down the hall.
- Reach out to a former mentor or that one teacher who always seems to have a new idea brewing.

Growth doesn't have to come with a name badge and hotel lanyard. It can look like collaboration, curiosity, and carving out a little space for your own professional joy right where you are.

CHAPTER 15

Becoming Better Without Burning Out

How do you grow in teaching when the tools or support don't seem to exist?

Teaching is one of those rare professions where you never stop growing, and that's what makes it so incredible. It's not about being perfect; it's about staying curious, exploring new ideas, and finding ways to make your life in the classroom easier, rewarding, and sustainable. Leaning into growth is one way to make that happen. Every teacher, no matter how experienced, has room to refine their craft, and that's a beautiful thing. Leaning into growth isn't about fixing what's broken, it's about giving yourself permission to reflect, refine, and rediscover what makes teaching feel purposeful. As a matter of fact, "The more professional development teachers get, the more likely students are to succeed."[1] Teachers deserve access to the kind of tools and support that help them feel confident, capable, and a little less stressed. However, having access to ongoing learning opportunities is not a reality for all teachers. Unfortunately, ongoing professional development isn't a guarantee in every school, but that doesn't mean you can't still grow.

---

[1] Robinson, Java. "Why Professional Development Matters." *NEA*, February 11, 2019. https://www.nea.org/professional-excellence/student-engagement/tools-tips/why-professional-development-matters.

In-House Talent

What can schools do when there's no budget for instructional coaches or national conferences? Meaningful professional development doesn't always require a plane ticket or a big price tag. While my school has the resources to send teachers to conferences, our school leaders also know how to maximize the talent already in the building. They identify teachers who have strong instructional skills or unique areas of expertise and invite them to lead peer-based professional development. These teacher-led sessions are often more relevant and engaging because they're created by people who understand our students and school culture. Sometimes it's a workshop. Other times it's a model lesson or a collaborative planning session, but no matter the format, the goal is the same: to share practical strategies, swap ideas that work, and grow together in ways that make sense for our classrooms.

So, what does peer-led professional development look like in our school? Picture a mini conference, right on campus, built into one of our professional learning days. This event typically includes breakout sessions where teachers present on various topics such as differentiated instruction, classroom technology integration, or student engagement strategies. By utilizing its own teachers as PD leaders and hosting a mini conference, our school fosters a culture of continuous learning and professional growth. This approach not only empowers educators but also strengthens our sense of community, ensuring that professional development remains practical, relevant, and directly applicable to classroom success. At our school, teachers who volunteer to lead a session get a free period built into their day to either prep, catch up on work, or just take a breather. It's a simple structure that makes professional learning more personal and far more effective.

Always Learning

As educators, we are always on the lookout for new strategies, tools, and resources to improve our teaching, but some of the most powerful opportunities for growth don't come from a conference or a curriculum, they come from within. Taking the time to reflect on our own practices helps us identify areas where we can grow and refine our skills. By adopting a mindset of continuous learning, we can try out new methods, ask for feedback from peers, and adjust our approaches to better meet the ever-changing needs of our students. Growth isn't just about attending workshops, training sessions, or earning certificates. It's about developing self-awareness and being willing to step outside our comfort zones. When we take the time to look inward, we discover our full potential dedicated to making a meaningful difference. After all these years in education, I can honestly say there hasn't been a single year where I didn't uncover something I could improve upon, and that, to me, is the beauty of teaching. It's a career that grows with you, as long as you're willing to keep growing with it.

You Must Be Mistaken...

A while ago I found myself on the receiving end of a classic parent complaint, and it ended up being a major growth moment for me. As a gifted education teacher, one of the most common concerns I hear from parents is, "My child is bored in their general education classroom; therefore, they should be in your gifted education class." In my district, students need to take a series of assessments and score within a certain range to become eligible and receive gifted education services. When students don't meet those scores, parents often come to me, hoping to share stories about how their child is bored in their general education classroom and why they believe their child needs gifted services. Over and over, I find myself reassuring parents that my colleagues are fully capable of teaching all students, no matter their ability or learning style. But this year, something unexpected happened; a parent told me that her son found *my* class boring.

Steven had been in my class for just three days (and let's not forget, I only see my students once a week). She messaged me asking about his progress. As a new student in the gifted program, Steven was experiencing a bit of a learning curve. I am always happy to communicate with parents about their child's progress, so I messaged Steven's mom back saying, "Steven is doing quite well; he is experiencing a bit of a learning curve which is to be expected as he is new to the gifted program. However, I am confident that with time and some one-on-one help, he'll become proficient as the year progresses." She responded immediately, "Well Steven says he's bored in your class. Maybe you should try more hands-on learning like building with LEGO if you want him to be more engaged and successful."

Me? The high-energy, pun-loving, LEGO-building, laugh-until-we-learn teacher? Boring? Surely, she had the wrong classroom. I practically had my rebuttal locked and loaded: "You must be thinking of someone else. I'm the one with the joke of the day and logic puzzles disguised as fun." I was ready to go to battle. After writing about ten defensive replies, I finally did something unexpected. I left her message unanswered. She had asked about her son's progress, and I had already given a thoughtful, professional response. I decided to set a boundary, prioritize my mental health, and step away from the back-and-forth, but the message didn't really go away. It just replayed in my head on a loop: "My son is bored. Your class is boring."

I checked in with Steven's homeroom teacher, hoping this was all just a misunderstanding. With a knowing smile, she said, "Oh yeah, that mom? She told me the same thing. He's bored in my class too," and just like that I felt validated. I'll admit, my instinct was to take my solidarity and clap back with one of my favorite teacher quotes: "Boredom is a choice. People with imaginations are never bored," but instead of reacting, I paused. I stayed in that pause for a good week or two, letting the discomfort sink in. Eventually, I started asking myself the harder questions: Why is he bored? Is he confused by the content? Is he feeling isolated? What might I be missing? That's when it clicked. This wasn't about defending my teaching style. It was about understanding his experience and figuring out how to meet him where he was.

The following week, I made a conscious decision to shift gears and be more intentional with my teaching. I focused on increasing student talk, encouraging more collaboration, and finding every excuse possible to get kids up and moving, because nothing says engagement like giving young students engaged in conversations without teacher control. I started paying closer attention to Steven. I noticed he'd been sitting alone by choice, not because of anything disciplinary. I casually paired him with a classmate, Molly, who can happily talk to a box of pencils, and within minutes, he and Molly were chumming it up so much that I had to redirect them during instruction time. By the end of class, I wasn't sure if the shift had truly made a difference, but as we were walking back to his homeroom class, Steven looked up at me, completely unprompted, and said, **"Your class is so much fun. Thursdays are my favorite day of the week."** Y'all. I nearly melted right there in the hallway. All I could think was: *Yes! This is why I was born to teach.*

And guess what? The next day, the unthinkable happened. I got a message from his mom: "I don't know what you did, but Steven absolutely loves your class and can't wait until next week." I fought the urge to respond, "Oh, you mean the boring class?" and instead typed, "I knew he would settle in. Sometimes it just takes a few weeks. I look forward to an amazing year."

Now, did I completely overhaul my entire teaching style because of one parent's comment? Absolutely not, but no matter how effective or experienced we are, especially those of us who've been in the game for a while, it's always okay to look for ways to grow. Sometimes, it's the smallest adjustments that make the biggest impact. This experience reminded me that even when we feel confident in our teaching, there's still room to stretch. Growth doesn't mean throwing everything out and starting over. It means being open to reflection, willing to try something new, and staying responsive to the students right in front of us, because growth isn't just for our students. It's for us, too. So, the next time you hear a comment that stings a little, take a breath. Reflect, and ask yourself, "What can I learn from this?" You might just discover a better way to connect with a student, or better yet, you may even reignite a spark for teaching.

I know we've all encountered those parents who overuse the my-child-is-bored sentiment as a way to excuse their child's behavior or performance in the classroom. While it's important to reflect on our practices and adjust when needed, it's equally important to recognize when boredom is being used as an excuse rather than a genuine concern. So, I want to share a few responses for those moments when you need to gently, or not so gently, push back and help parents see the bigger picture.

When a parent repeatedly claims, "My child is bored in your class! That's why he/she ______," consider factoring in variations of the following in your response:

- Curious kids are usually never bored because they're too busy asking, "What if?" and "Why not?" while the bored ones are still stuck on, "Do I have to?"

- Boredom can sometimes be a signal that a student needs a challenge, but it can also mean they're being asked to work through something that takes a little more effort. Let's explore which one this is.

- Boredom is the brain's way of saying, "I'm too lazy to be curious right now."

- I always take student feedback seriously, and I'll be sure to keep a close eye on your child's level of engagement. That said, part of learning includes encouraging persistence with tasks that may not be instantly exciting but are still valuable for critical thinking and growth. I'll continue supporting them in both skill-building and enjoyment.

- Boredom is usually a choice, and sometimes, it's a clever one. But I'm here to help your child find more meaningful ways to stretch that big brain of theirs.

- I completely understand wanting your child to feel excited about learning. When students mention they're bored, it's often less about the lesson itself and more about how they're engaging with the material. I'm happy to look at ways we can better support their learning needs while also encouraging responsibility and curiosity in the classroom.

One of the biggest lessons I've learned as a teacher is that engagement isn't a one-way street. It's a reminder that engagement and curiosity often come down to a child's mindset. While we, as educators, strive to create dynamic and meaningful learning experiences, students also play a role in their own engagement. It's a partnership. Of course, this doesn't mean we dismiss concerns outright. Instead, it's an opportunity to open a dialogue with parents about how we can work together to foster their child's curiosity, resilience, and love of learning. Sometimes, the conversation shifts from

"Your class is boring" to "How can we help your child take ownership of their learning?" This shift in perspective can make all the difference for the student, the parent, and even for us as teachers.

You don't need a fancy conference to experience that kind of renewal. Inspiration is everywhere if you know where to look. Start in your own building. That teacher down the hall with a classroom that somehow never feels chaotic. Ask them how they do it. Host a mini-PD with your team. Pick a topic, grab snacks, and talk about what works. The best professional development isn't always formal. Sometimes it looks like a hallway chat that turns into a lightbulb moment, and let's talk about your phone. Yes, the one that makes you want to scream when it pings with another email. That same device is a treasure trove of free professional growth. Podcasts, Instagram reels, TikTok tips, YouTube channels are full of brilliant educators out there sharing gold for free. Find them. Follow them. Get to know them. Learn from them. Let them remind you why you started.

CHAPTER 16

Finding Value in Creative Thinking

When was the last time curiosity took over your classroom, and what did that look like for both you and your students?

Although it can be frustrating to hear students and sometimes their parents complain that "school is boring," they may have a point. The truth is many kids are bored not because they lack discipline or drive, but because schools often fail to capture their imagination. Too often, schools prioritize listening to lectures, memorizing facts for tests, and completing worksheets that feel disconnected from real life thus draining the excitement out of learning.

Children are born curious. They are natural explorers, question-askers, and idea-generators, yet somewhere along the way, that curiosity is stifled by systems more focused on control than creativity. If we want students to be engaged, we have to rethink what school looks like. We have to build classrooms where wonder, relevance, and imagination aren't side notes, they're the starting point. We must make learning feel meaningful, relevant, and alive.

In an age driven by data and standardized assessments, it's easy for educators to focus primarily on facts, formulas, and test scores. However, our role as educators goes far beyond academic data points. Educators should strive to develop young minds that can think critically, solve problems, and adapt to an ever-changing world. While data helps us measure progress and achievement, it fails to define the full scope of student potential. Real learning happens when students move beyond memorization and engage in the kind of thinking that fosters innovation, curiosity, and resilience. When we embrace creative thinking in the classroom, we give students the confidence to explore ideas, take intellectual risks, and build knowledge in ways that extend far beyond the limits of any textbook or test.

Full STEAM

Remember Mrs. Edwards, my senior AP English teacher? She was incorporating the elements of STEAM education before it was even a recognized educational philosophy. According to Herron, "STEAM education has its roots in STEM, which was first popularized in the early 2000s by Dr. Judith Ramaley, a former director of the National Science Foundation (NSF)…The Rhode Island School of Design (RISD) was one of the first institutions to advocate for this shift from STEM to STEAM around 2011. They believed that design and creativity play a critical role in innovation and should be at the forefront of education. RISD's approach quickly caught on, and the idea of STEAM spread globally."[1] Mrs. Edwards was clearly ahead of her time.

Mrs. Edwards believed in the power of creativity and imagination, thus making learning genuinely fun. Even with the pressure of looming AP exams, she didn't overwhelm us with test-taking strategies or endless drills. Instead, she created a relaxed and joyful atmosphere where her students engaged in meaningful and rich discussions. Mrs. Edwards helped her students develop a genuine love for English literature while subtly preparing us for the AP exam through deep understanding and critical thinking. I'll never forget how Mrs. Edwards turned Edith Hamilton's *Mythology* into a real-life STEAM experience.[2]

---

[1] "Let's Talk About It Tuesday: What Is STEAM Education, And Where Did It Come From?," January 28, 2025. https://www.code313detroit.org/lets-talk-about-it-tuesday-what-is-steam-education-and-where-did-it-come-from#:~:text = Where%20Did%20STEAM%20Education%20Originate,National%20Science%20Foundation%20(NSF).

[2] Hamilton, Edith. *Mythology: Timeless Tales of Gods and Heroes.* New York: Little, Brown and Company, 1942.

Mrs. Edwards got approval from administration, and before long our class was sketching, planning, and painting a mural on the back wall of our classroom. We begged Mrs. Edwards to stay after school so we could work on the mural. Once complete, we wrote versions of Greek mythology, and then we invited 8th graders into our classroom where we acted as docents and took turns bringing ancient stories to life through our own words. We explained everything from the origin of the universe to the rise of the gods and the creation of humanity. I told the story of Persephone and Demeter, the myth behind the changing seasons, and I remember it as clearly as if I told it yesterday.

Here's a breakdown of the elements of STEAM education as applied to *Mythology: Timeless Tales of Gods and Heroes* by Edith Hamilton:

Science (S): Color Theory: We explored how different colors can make people feel and what they often represent, like how red is tied to bravery or passion, and how blue is often linked to wisdom or calm. Then we got into the science side of things, breaking down what's in paint. We compared acrylic and oil paints, looked at what makes them dry faster or slower, and talked about how certain ingredients can change the texture, shine, and even how long the paint lasts.

Technology (T): Projection and Scaling: We used a digital projector to blow up our mural design onto the wall so we could trace it with the right proportions. It was kind of like high-tech coloring book outlines. It made painting way easier and helped us keep all the tiny details in check. Now, this all happened back in 1990, so while today's students can pull up designs on tablets and use laser levels, we were over here making magic with overhead projectors and determination. We did not have fancy tools, but we made use of what we had.

Engineering (E): Wall Preparation and Materials: Before we picked up a single paintbrush, we had to think like engineers and artists. We figured out how to prep the wall so our masterpiece wouldn't peel, fade, or flake off in a week. Then we had to determine what type of paint would survive teenage fingerprints and years of classroom chaos. We went with paints tough enough to last but bold enough to pop. This wasn't just a mural; it was built to survive high school.

Arts (A): Creative Expression: This was the heart and soul of the project. We didn't just learn about mythology; we brought it to life using everything from bold brushstrokes to creative composition. We turned ancient legends into eye-catching visual stories. Heroes, monsters, and gods all showed up on the wall, thanks to thoughtful symbolism, clever color choices, and some serious storytelling skills. To pull it off, we divided the mural into sections. Some parts were solo missions, others were team efforts but all of it came together in one powerful, unified piece. Every student had a voice, every idea had a place, and by the end, what started as scattered sketches turned into a mural that felt epic enough to belong in Olympus.

Mathematics (M): Scaling and Proportion: Before we could paint anything, we had to put our math hats on. Using grid systems and ratios, we scaled our designs to fit the giant wall. We turned tiny sketches into larger-than-life scenes. Then came the real-world problem-solving. We had to figure out just how much paint and materials we'd need without blowing the budget. We crunched numbers, measured the wall, and calculated everything from surface area to supply costs. Turns out, murals require more than creativity. They also demand serious math skills, teamwork, and maybe a calculator or two.

I scored a two out of five on the AP English exam. According to the College Board, "a two is not a good AP score, as it is not considered passing. If you earn a two on your AP exam, it might be better not to submit that score to colleges."[3] So yeah, I may have "failed" my AP English exam, but thanks to teachers like Mrs. Edwards, I developed a love for creative thinking and learning. For me, it's the teachers who teach beyond the data and make learning meaningful that truly inspire and change lives regardless of test scores.

---

[3] Parker, Bethanny. "What Is a Good AP Score?" Bestcolleges.com, August 15, 2022. https://www.bestcolleges.com/blog/what-is-good-ap-score/.

I am not saying that data and test scores have no place in education. Of course they do. Teachers use data to improve instruction and learning outcomes. Data helps us track progress, pinpoint areas where students are struggling, and adjust our teaching to meet individual needs. On a larger scale, schools can also use data to evaluate the effectiveness of programs and policies, ensuring resources are allocated efficiently. Ultimately, data can empower schools to create more equitable, effective, and student-centered learning environments. However, while data can be an effective tool for improving educational outcomes, schools should not make data the primary focus.

When test scores become the only thing schools focus on, we start to lose the soul of education, because let's be real, learning isn't just about numbers on a spreadsheet. It's about curiosity, creativity, connection, and growth. Yes, data has its place, but it's not the whole story. Kids are more than their scores, and teaching is more than hitting a benchmark. If we over-focus on measurable outcomes, we risk overlooking what really matters: the spark in a student's eye when they finally "get it," the quiet confidence that grows after a tough concept clicks, or the joy of creating something they're proud of. Teachers know that. We know our students and not just their academic levels. We know their quirks, their struggles, their talents, and their dreams. That kind of insight doesn't come from a data chart, it comes from showing up, day after day, and truly paying attention.

The Genius of Amplifying Student Voices

How do you make space for students' voices in your classroom?

In a classroom centered on data and student achievement, the teacher's voice often dominates the learning experience through guiding discussions, setting expectations, and delivering content. But what happens when we shift the focus and allow students to actively participate in shaping their own education? What if we create an environment where their ideas, questions, and choices influence the learning process? Imagine a classroom as a community of thinkers, creators, and collaborators.

When educators create spaces for meaningful dialogue, choice, and collaboration, students thrive. Students who feel seen become more engaged, motivated, and invested in their learning. Their sense of ownership increases, leading to deeper understanding and a stronger connection to the material. Amplifying student voices doesn't mean taking a step back in the classroom, it means creating classroom norms that incorporate student-led discussions and designing projects that allow for personalized and authentic learning. By embracing a student-centered approach, we can transform our classrooms into dynamic spaces where learners are empowered to think critically, advocate for themselves, and take charge of a lifelong educational journey.

Let's explore how to make student voices not just heard, but truly valued. People often ask how I manage to stay so positive about teaching. The truth is I don't always. Like every teacher, I hit rough patches. I call these my "teaching slumps." When that happens, I turn to the people who know the work best: other educators. As a teacher surrounded by incredible colleagues and a mom of two kids who've had their share of amazing teachers, I'm lucky to be part of a vibrant, inspiring community. I always tell folks, "My best ideas come from other teachers."

Before I share how Ms. Ford helped transform my son from "I hate school! School is the worst place in the world!" to "Mom, you're not going to believe what I did in school today," I need to give you a little background on my son, Fox, during this time.

Titanic Obsession

Fox is eight and lives and breathes the Titanic. From the moment he wakes up, his mind is filled with facts about the ship; how long it was, how many rivets held it together, the names of its most famous passengers. His bedroom is a shrine to the doomed ocean liner, covered in posters, books, and a carefully built model that he refuses to let anyone touch. At school, he sneaks Titanic trivia into every subject, turning math problems into an iceberg collision and writing stories about passengers in language arts. Our family humors his obsession, listening patiently as he recites yet another theory about the ship's sinking over dinner. While other kids race around at recess, Fox wonders what it must have felt like on that cold April night in 1912 literally reenacting the tragedy. Some call it an obsession, but for Fox, the Titanic isn't just a ship, it's a world he can dive into, explore, and understand in a way that makes him feel connected to something bigger than himself.

When Fox was about to begin third grade with Ms. Ford, I gave her a heads-up about two things: his deep obsession with the Titanic and his equally strong dislike for school. Both a colleague and friend, Ms. Ford looked at me with care and experience and offered a gentle reassurance that I understood. At that moment, I knew my child was in the right hands. About a month into the school year, Ms. Ford sent me an eight-minute video clip of Fox literally teaching his entire class about the Titanic and its sister ships using a Google Slide presentation he had created. During his presentation, complete with a teacher pointer stick, Fox taught confidently and proudly. His classmates leaned in, asked questions, and responded with genuine interest, clearly captivated by Fox's knowledge and enthusiasm. It wasn't just a presentation; it was an impact that would last forever.

Ms. Ford isn't just a great teacher; she is a confident one. I imagine an administrator questioning her during a formal observation, "Why are you letting a student teach a mini lesson on the Titanic to the class? That's not part of the third-grade curriculum!" I picture Ms. Ford calmly and professionally replying, "You're right, the Titanic isn't one of the 3rd grade standards, but do you know what is? Informational text is. When you come in with your clipboard to observe me, you can't measure the kind of impact I'm making on that child. Not everything that matters fits in your observation rubric." I can't speak for Ms. Ford, nor our administration for that matter, but I suspect that many readers would be hesitant to go off script for fear of being poorly evaluated.

People love to say that kids are like sponges and they soak everything up, and personally I agree. However, here's the thing about sponges: if you squeeze them hard enough, everything leaks out. I think the impact great teachers have on kids is more like that old stain on a classroom ceiling. You might not remember exactly how it got there or when it happened, but you know it's there to stay. That's the kind of lasting impression educators like Ms. Ford make every day whether it's captured on a data wall or not.

Genius Hour How-To

My mom-heart exploded with joy as I watched my son passionately teach his classmates about the Titanic and other ships, but my teacher-brain could not help but admire Ms. Ford's wisdom and expertise. Often teachers assign projects where students are asked to present, but this was more like an impromptu "Genius Hour." Genius hour is "based on the concept that people have ideas and solutions to their own problems and are able to bring those ideas and solutions to life with the proper guidance and resources." Using Genius Hour in a classroom allows students an opportunity to explore a particular area of interest. "This can be anything from exploring a new hobby or interest, to working on a solution to a problem they've been having. The sky is the limit."[1]

In a school system often dominated by standardized tests and strict lesson plans, Genius Hour carves out space for creativity, innovation, and self-directed learning. When students are given the freedom to explore ideas that excite them, they become more engaged, more motivated, and more invested in their learning.

To host a Genius Hour, you don't need to overhaul your entire schedule. Begin by setting aside a consistent time each week. You can start with one hour on Fridays or a few minutes after recess. Introduce the concept by explaining that students will have the freedom to choose a topic they're curious about and then create a project centered

---

[1] Strobel, Kim. "Exploring Genius Hour: Projects Ideas, Benefits, and Tips for Maximizing Learning | Strobel Education." *Strobel Education* (blog), August 17, 2023. https://strobeleducation.com/blog/exploring-genius-hour/.

around that interest. It could be anything from inventing a new game, learning how to code, researching endangered species, building a model of a dream city, or like Fox, the Titanic. The only requirement is that their project involves research, learning something new, and sharing what they've learned with others.

Early on, help students narrow their interests into open-ended questions using prompts like "How might I..." or "What would happen if..." to guide their inquiry. Throughout the process, provide checkpoints to keep them organized and on track. These might include a project proposal, a timeline, a brief research summary, and a final product or presentation. Some students may prefer to work independently, while others might thrive in pairs or small groups, depending on your classroom dynamic. Be sure to build in reflection time, allowing students to think about what they've learned, what challenges they faced, and what they're proud of. This reflective component helps students connect their Genius Hour experience to broader learning goals and personal growth. Genius Hour is not just about creating a product; it's about fostering a mindset. It shows students that their ideas matter and that learning can be driven by curiosity. It shows them that their passions have a place in the classroom. For teachers, it's a beautiful reminder of why we teach in the first place: to inspire our students to explore, discover, and become confident in who they are.

Genius Hour is about integrating real-world skills where students learn how to research, manage their time, problem-solve, and adapt when things don't go as planned. It teaches students to take risks, embrace failure as part of the process, and develop a growth mindset. For teachers, it's more than just handing over time for exploration. Genius Hour empowers students to take ownership of their learning just like Ms. Ford did with Fox. When students are given the chance to explore their passions, they don't just meet expectations, they exceed them. For more, I recommend: *Genius Hour: Passion Projects That Ignite Innovation and Student Inquiry* by Andi McNair.[2]

---

[2] McNair, Andi. *Genius Hour: Passion Projects That Ignite Innovation and Student Inquiry*. 2nd ed. Waco, TX: Prufrock Press, 2022.

As I write this book, I can proudly say that Fox performed well on his end-of-year Georgia Milestones tests. It was his first time taking a full grade-level assessment, and thanks to Ms. Ford's guidance, and her magical ability to spark curiosity without turning up the pressure, he walked in calm and confident. More important than test scores, she gave Fox a genuine love of learning that no standardized test can ever measure.

In the end, Fox's test scores were a nice affirmation, but they weren't the real win. The real win was hearing him come home every day, bubbling with excitement about what he learned. It was watching him walk into school not with dread, but with anticipation. It was seeing his curiosity not just accepted but celebrated. *That's what happens when a teacher sees the student* before *the standard*. When a child's passion isn't treated as a distraction, but as a doorway to deeper learning, true magic unfolds. Ms. Ford didn't just teach content. She taught Fox that his voice matters. She reminded me, and hopefully reminds all of us, what can happen when we let students take the lead, when we let their passions guide us instead of always guiding them. While there's no standardized way to capture that kind of magic, you'll know it when you see it. It lingers. Like the best kind of learning.

Finding Mentors in Unlikely Places

Who at your school inspires you, and how might you use that inspiration in your classroom?

Teaching can be an isolating profession at times. We move through our days with our heads down, juggling lesson plans, parent emails, and the million little moments that make up classroom life. In the rush, we often forget to look up and see the brilliance happening right down the hall. I've had the privilege of working alongside many talented educators throughout my career, including the incredible Ms. Ford, but had my son, Fox, not landed in her third-grade class, I may have missed the extraordinary magic unfolding in her room. It's not a lack of interest that keeps us from noticing; it's the sheer weight of our own responsibilities that sometimes blinds us to the inspiration within our own schools.

Even though it's easy to stay in my lane and focus solely on my own teaching obligations, I've come to appreciate the power of having an unofficial mentor. This is the kind of mentorship that grows organically and is rooted in mutual respect and shared experiences. Having an experienced teacher to guide you through challenges, celebrate your wins, and offer support when things feel overwhelming can make all the difference. A great mentor is more than someone who answers questions; they're a sounding board, a problem solver, and a steady source of encouragement. They've walked the same halls, faced similar struggles, and offer a kind of insight and empathy that others simply may not understand.

Mentorship isn't just about survival. It's about growth. Learning from someone who has been in your shoes helps you **build confidence, refine your teaching practices, and develop a deeper understanding of your school's culture**. A mentor can share time-saving strategies, help navigate school politics, and remind you that perfection and test scores are not always the goal. Mentorship isn't just for new teachers; even seasoned educators like me can benefit from having a trusted colleague to bounce ideas off. The best teachers never stop learning, and having a mentor (or becoming one) keeps the cycle of support and growth alive in a school community.

People often look to me for inspiration and positive energy, but even folks like me, folks who love teaching, end up in the teacher's lounge complaining about challenging students, broken Chromebooks, endless meetings, paperwork, difficult parents, and so on. Sometimes we need to vent to get through the day, and when I find myself in a teacher slump, I turn to my "unofficial" mentors. In fact, one mentor has no idea that she is even my mentor, and unless she reads this book, she may never realize the impact that she has on both her students and colleagues.

It didn't take much effort for me to find an unofficial mentor in my son's photography teacher, Ms. Hewitt. Jackson, my 10-year-old math whiz, has a love-hate relationship with school. He sees numbers differently. He doesn't just solve math problems; he knows the answers before most kids have finished reading the question, and often to the frustration of many of his teachers, he's usually right. He refuses to show his work, not out of defiance, but because he genuinely doesn't understand why he needs to show his work. "It's just obvious," he says, shrugging. Beyond numbers, Jackson's interests are an interesting mix of video games, gardening, and, until recently, not much else. Imaginative play? Nope. Storytelling? Not his thing. Even when his kindergarten teachers encouraged students to dress up as their future career, Jackson stood firm: "I don't know what I want to be when I grow up. I like being a kid." He has a point. Maybe we should stop rushing childhood and let kids just be kids, but I digress. He describes school as long, repetitive, and full of assignments that seem unnecessary in his eyes. "Why is my math class an hour long when it only takes me five minutes to do the work?" I don't always have a good answer for him, but then something extraordinary happened. Jackson enrolled in Ms. Hewitt's photography class.

Starting in fourth grade, students at our school get to choose their enrichment classes. In addition to photography, our elementary school offers robotics, dance, theater, orchestra, Spanish, and engineering. When it came time to make his selections, Jackson had one clear goal: avoid PE and dance at all costs. So, he chose photography.

For an entire year, he never shared anything about this class. Then one afternoon, he came home absolutely glowing. Ms. Hewitt had invited him and a couple of friends to eat lunch in her classroom. To Jackson, this wasn't just a lunch invitation, it was a lifeline. She saw him. She tapped into his curiosity, sparked his creativity, and created a space where he could breathe, explore, and just be. In her room, Jackson didn't need to show his work. Jackson found a safe space, and all he needed to do was show up as himself.

Now, I'm not suggesting teachers give up their much-needed lunch breaks. I'm simply sharing the magic that comes from a real connection. Jackson didn't fall in love with photography, but he found his place at school because he found a teacher who made him feel seen. By the end of fourth grade, Jackson was excited to sign up for photography in the fifth grade as one of his enrichment classes. Photography with Ms. Hewitt became his favorite part of the day. For a kid who had spent most of his school years watching the clock and counting the minutes to freedom, that class? That class was different simply because Ms. Hewitt had made a real connection. The next year, Ms. Hewitt introduced him to bubble photography. He came home and launched into a full-blown explanation about macro photography, abstract art, exposure, and uncooperative subjects. Turns out, bubbles don't always cooperate. Who knew? I sat there listening in awe, realizing it was the first time he had ever spoken about school with that kind of energy and enthusiasm.

Then, midway through fifth grade, while we were riding in the car, Jackson suddenly looked over at me and asked, "Mama, do you think I could be a photographer when I grow up?" I glanced at him, catching that rare spark of possibility in his eyes, and smiled. "Absolutely, son. I think you'd be an amazing photographer. The world is yours." My little boy. The boy who had never shared a dream of adulthood looked at me with a glimmer of hope in his eyes imagining a world where he could grow up and become a photographer all because Ms. Hewitt made a connection with him. Sometimes it simply takes one class, one teacher, or one unexpected passion for a kid to see themselves in a way they had never imagined.

Ms. Hewitt didn't just teach photography; she taught confidence, curiosity, and the power of belonging. I never scheduled a meeting or filled out a mentorship form, but through simple moments, casual conversations, and in the quiet reassurance that what we do matters beyond the data, Ms. Hewitt is my unexpected mentor. She is the type of teacher that both her students and colleagues will remember, and for that, I am endlessly grateful.

Of course, I've told Ms. Hewitt many times just how much of an impact she has had on Jackson, but sadly she will never be the teacher sitting in a school data meeting getting praised for "moving the needle." She will never see her name on a spreadsheet showing "growth" or "gains."

Creativity Can't be Standardized

There is no standardized test for sparking curiosity or helping a child find where they belong or unknowingly mentoring other teachers by leading by example.

The artists, the musicians, the theater directors, the robotics coaches, the media specialists, the PE teachers, and the world-language instructors are the educators who are transforming students in immeasurable ways. They ignite passions, build confidence, and give kids a reason to show up. Yet, too often, they are overlooked, undervalued, and unrecognized because their impact isn't easily measured in numbers. We celebrate the reading scores, the math benchmarks, and the percentage of students who "exceeded expectations," but what about the students who found their passion because of an elective teacher? What about the kids who never spoke in class until theater gave them a voice? What about the students who never saw themselves as talented until they picked up a paintbrush, a camera, or an instrument? We need to do better. We need to recognize these teachers not just with a passing "thank you," but with the same level of respect, appreciation, and acknowledgment as those in the core subjects. We need to highlight their stories, celebrate their impact, and fight for their programs to remain funded and prioritized.

Every teacher needs a mentor regardless of years in the field. These unofficial mentors are the educators who show up exactly when you need them most. Sometimes, the most meaningful mentorship doesn't happen in formal coaching sessions or structured professional development. Sometimes it happens by watching how a teacher greets each student by name or how they redirect with compassion instead of control. For me, it's casually seeing how Ms. Hewitt makes room for weirdness, creativity, and quiet kids who haven't yet found their way. Watching Ms. Hewitt with her students is like watching a masterclass in humanity. Without ever handing me a lesson plan or telling me what to do, she's modeled a way of teaching that feels both grounded and liberating. She reminds me that impact isn't always loud, and that the quiet magic we make in our classrooms matters.

CHAPTER 19

Create the Career You Desire

How do you stay passionate about teaching while also taking care of yourself?

Teaching is often described as a calling, but it's also a demanding career that requires skill, expertise, and fair compensation. Too often, educators are expected to sacrifice their well-being, time, and even financial stability under the guise of "doing it for the kids," but passion alone won't pay the bills, prevent burnout, or ensure long-term career fulfillment. If we want to thrive rather than just survive, we must take ownership of our careers and make decisions that work best for us without experiencing "teacher guilt."

For years, I thrived in the world of first and second grade where wiggly teeth, untied shoelaces, and spontaneous dance parties were part of the daily routine. I loved it, but deep down I was bored. I grew bored of teaching the same curriculum in a way that felt forced and micromanaged. A quiet voice had been nudging me toward something more. I had seen the spark in my brightest students, the ones who asked questions I didn't always have answers to, who made connections far beyond their years, who craved something deeper, richer. I wanted to be the teacher who gave them that. I wanted to be the teacher who saw them, challenged them, and let them soar, so I hunkered down for a year and obtained my Gifted Education Endorsement while working full time as a second-grade teacher.

As luck would have it, a gifted position opened the following year at my school, and I knew this was finally my time to shine. I had the passion, the drive, and the experience. I poured my heart into my application, rehearsed every possible interview question, and visualized myself stepping into that classroom, finally doing what I had dreamed of for years, but in the end I didn't get the job. I was devastated, and I wanted to quit.

By the next week, the disappointment had settled into something clearer. If my school wasn't going to see my potential as a gifted teacher, then I had two choices: stay where I was and hope for another opportunity or take charge of my own career and design my own journey. I popped into my principal's office and said, "I need to tell you something. I'm going to pursue gifted education. I really like working at our school. I love our community. I love the culture, and I love working for you, but if there is not a gifted position for me here in an upcoming year or two, I am going to start exploring positions at other schools." I explained that I wanted to be a lifelong teacher; however, I needed to develop my career in such a way that feels passionate for me just as she had pursued administration. I approached this respectfully and professionally, but I also made it known that I intended to do what's best for my career.

Within a couple of weeks, I discovered a gifted position at a nearby school. I submitted my resume, interviewed, and the principal offered me a position on the spot, but I hesitated. I asked her to give me a week and she agreed. The following day I went into my principal's office and told her about the offer. I explained that I was torn, because "I really like working here, but I want to pursue gifted education." She said, "Give me one more year. I'll create a gifted position if I must because you belong here." And just like that I had negotiated a position for myself. I had no idea that negotiating a teaching position was even an option, but there I was sitting across from my principal making a case for a role that didn't technically exist. I expected a hard no or at least some bureaucratic pushback, but instead, my principal listened. In that moment, I realized something powerful: sometimes, in education, we wait for permission when we should be advocating for what's best for us. I walked into that meeting unsure of my own leverage, and I walked out having shaped my own journey.

Becoming a gifted education teacher wasn't just about landing a new job, it was about learning to fight for my own career. It was about realizing that if I want something badly enough, I may have to be willing to walk away from what is comfortable. It is about trusting myself even when others don't see my potential right away. Teachers spend our days advocating for our students and pushing them to dream big and reach higher, and sometimes we need to take our own advice and follow our dreams.

Teachers are often expected to give endlessly without ever looking up to ask, "What do I want from this career?" Teaching is a profession, not a vow of self-sacrifice. You are allowed to grow, shift, and seek out new opportunities that align with your passions, strengths, and goals. Whether that means stepping into leadership, presenting at conferences, launching a creative side project, or simply setting boundaries that protect your peace, your career should work for you and not just the system you're working in.

There's sometimes a quiet pressure in education to stay in the same lane forever and prove your dedication by staying put, but career advancement doesn't mean you care less about kids; it means you're honoring your own growth while continuing to make a difference. It's not abandoning the classroom or your students, it's expanding your influence. So don't apologize for wanting more. Advocate for yourself the way you advocate for your students: boldly, unapologetically, and with your future in mind.

CHAPTER 20

Protecting Your Peace One Parent at a Time

When was the last time you stood firm in what you believed, and how did that moment impact you and your students?

Teachers are encouraged to advocate for our students, our schools, and for the heart of education, but advocating for ourselves is not always easy. We're taught to be team players, to put others first, to make do with what we're given, and to do it for the kids. We're told that teaching is a calling, and somewhere along the way, that has been twisted into the idea that asking for support, setting boundaries, or standing up for ourselves makes us less dedicated. However, when we stand up for ourselves, we aren't just protecting our well-being, we're ensuring we have the energy, passion, and longevity to continue making an impact.

Too often, I witness teachers, and even administrators, afraid to stand up to angry parents. We're afraid of the potential backlash, but as educators, we are the experts in our classrooms, and it's essential that we advocate for what's best for our students and ourselves even when facing pushback. Standing firm in our professional knowledge isn't about defiance; it's about protecting the integrity of our teaching and ensuring that every child gets what they truly need. Parents may have opinions, but we have expertise, so trust yourself, speak with confidence, and don't be afraid to set boundaries like I did with the PTA President at my school.

Nearly ten years into my teaching career, I received an unexpected request from our PTA president. She wasn't just any involved parent, she was "that" parent. She was the parent who knew every teacher's reputation and had a clear vision of where her child needed to be, and, according to her, that place was in my second-grade classroom. "I just know you're the best fit," she gushed, smiling as if we were old friends. "Everyone wants their kid in your second-grade class." "I have no say in placements. That's above my paygrade," I explained, and I naively thought that was the end of the story.

About three weeks later, my principal called me into her office. "We're moving the PTA president's son into your class," she said.

"Wait! what? Are you kidding me? Why?"

"She requested it," my principal continued. "She was insistent that you are the best teacher for him. She pulled a few strings, and, well... here we are."

I sighed but accepted my fate. I wasn't new to the politics of school placements, and I certainly wasn't new to parents maneuvering to get their children into certain classrooms. If she believed I was the right teacher, I'd welcome her child just like any other. For a while, it was fine. Her son was a bright and eager learner. He adjusted quickly and seemed happy in my class. Everything was running smoothly, but then, nearly halfway through the year, she requested a conference.

"We need to talk about homework, or in this case, the lack thereof." She sat across from me; arms crossed. "I've noticed that my child isn't bringing home any homework. When are you going to start giving him homework?"

I shared my homework philosophy and explained that research goes both ways with assigning homework in elementary school. However, I align with the notion that children have only one childhood, so I'd rather my students spend time reading with their families, exploring their interests, and simply being kids after school. She wasn't having it. "That's ridiculous. High-achieving students need to be challenged both at school and at home. You're setting them up for failure if you don't push them harder." I firmly reiterated my stance, backed by research, but she left in frustration saying that I didn't care about challenging my students.

Then, the whispers started. Other parents began asking me why I "refused" to give homework, and it didn't take long to trace the source. She had started telling people that I was lazy, that I didn't push my students, and that I was doing them a disservice. I could have ignored it, but this wasn't just a parent expressing an opinion. This was our PTA president. She was someone who chose to represent our school. As the gossip continued to spread, I felt frustration and anger building, so I picked up the phone and called her directly.

"This is unacceptable," I told her. "You're entitled to your opinion of me, but respectfully I believe the PTA President should be supporting teachers and building us up, not tearing us down. If you want to gossip about me and share your opinions, please feel free to do so. However, if you're going to choose to represent our school, please think about how your actions affect teachers, because I can assure you that I am not performing at my best because of how your actions have directly impacted me." She fumbled for a response, trying to downplay her words. "I just think parents have a right to our opinions."

"You do," I interrupted, "and I'm happy to discuss my teaching philosophy with anyone, but using your role in the PTA to turn people against a teacher? That's not advocacy; that's creating division when we should be working together for the best interest of our students." By the end of the year, her child had excelled, and he excelled without stacks of homework. While she never openly admitted it, I like to think that, deep down, she saw that learning isn't about quantity, it's about quality.

Some battles aren't really about homework. They're about control. They're about who gets to steer the conversation in education. Who gets to be heard and who gets to be dismissed. Too often, it's the loudest voices, not the wisest ones, that dominate the room. As teachers, our role isn't to please every parent or fold under pressure. Our job is to do what's right for all kids even when it's unpopular and even when it's misunderstood. Standing up for yourself isn't just self-preservation; it's advocacy for your classroom, your integrity, and your students, because at the end of the day, education shouldn't be about appeasement, it should be about purpose.

Administrators also play a vital role when it comes to standing up for teachers. I have worked with administrators who seem to cater to parents, but I have also had the opportunity to work for administrators who truly support their teachers. In this specific case, my principal supported me. Before I had a chance to spiral, my principal called me in. She didn't lecture or question my choices. Instead, she asked me to walk her through my reasoning. After I explained the research behind meaningful practice, my belief in protecting family time, and how I communicate expectations clearly with parents, she nodded and said, "You're the expert in your classroom. I trust you." She handled the parent directly, affirming my decision while offering the parent space to be heard. The parent continued to complain, but the support I felt from my administration made a huge impact, and that changed everything. It reminded me that when school leaders trust us and have our backs, we walk into classrooms with more confidence, and as a result, we're likely to stay in the profession longer.

Standing up to a parent doesn't mean being combative; it means being confident in your expertise and advocating for what's best for your students. There's a fine line between being defensive and being professional, and the key is knowing when to listen, when to clarify, and when to respectfully push back. You can honor a parent's perspective without compromising your values or instructional choices. Remember, you are the trained educator in the room. It's okay to say, "Here's why I made this decision," and trust that your knowledge and intent matter. When done with professionalism, empathy, and clarity, standing your ground isn't disrespectful; it's responsible.

CHAPTER 21

Have Fun and Teach Like Nobody's Watching

What would your teaching look like if no one was watching? What happens when you push the noise to the side and teach with your whole heart not to impress, not to prove, but simply because you love it? You know that feeling when the bell rings, and instead of feeling drained, you're still smiling? OK let's be real, you're likely drained and smiling, but is it the kind of day when your students didn't want to leave? That's the magic we're chasing. That's teaching like no one's watching. When was the last time you danced in your classroom? Sang a silly song? Made a mistake and laughed so hard with your students you cried a little? These moments, these real, unscripted, joy-filled moments are what make classrooms feel alive, and not only are they good for your soul, but they're also good for your students too.

One of the biggest fun-killers in teaching is the fear of judgment: from administration, colleagues, parents, and yes, sometimes even from our students and ourselves. But the best teachers aren't the ones who have perfectly laminated anchor charts or Pinterest-worthy classrooms. The best teachers are the ones who are real. Realness doesn't mean chaos. It doesn't mean a lack of structure or planning. It means showing up as your whole self, quirks, flaws, passions, and all and giving your students permission to do the same. It means ditching the mental performance review that plays on a loop in your head while asking, "If I weren't worried about what anyone thought, what would I do today?" Would you wear a costume to introduce a new book? Would you turn math into a scavenger hunt? Would you let your class build a city out of cardboard? Would you blast music while your students walk in, or rap your morning announcements? What would make your classroom authentic?

Let me say this clearly: you have full permission to bring that energy, that creativity, and that joy into your classroom, because not only is it allowed, it's exactly what your students need to thrive. Too many teachers are teaching from a place of fear. Fear of being misunderstood or fear of breaking the mold prevents us from truly tapping into our joy of teaching, or maybe it's the fear of that one email that says, "I heard about what you did today in class. . ." Fear-based teaching is exhausting. It dulls your creativity. It makes everything feel heavier than it needs to be, and it slowly chips away at the passion that brought you here in the first place, and if you're teaching from a place of joy, that's where you come alive again. Yes, someone might raise an eyebrow or two but finding the joy in teaching makes a far greater impact than a perfectly written objective on the board or achievement data.

Data is valuable and helps us measure students' progress and achievement. I am not saying that we should toss all data to the curb. I'm simply saying that prioritizing data over the whole child is killing the joy in schools for both kids and teachers alike. Imagine being a child sitting in today's classroom and failing to understand that your success solely centers around data points. Unfortunately, this is how most of us see learning and development. We often associate learning with rigor, structure, and quiet focus. While structure has its place, a growing body of research and real-world classroom experience shows that students learn best when they feel safe, relaxed, and emotionally connected.

Think about a time when you learned a new skill or concept. Let's take cooking for example. Imagine yourself, an adult, in a casual cooking class, apron on, music playing in the background, laughing over a slightly burnt batch of cookies. In that relaxed environment, you're more open to experimenting, asking questions, and trying a new technique without the fear of judgment or failure. The focus shifts from "doing it right" to "enjoying the learning," which helps the skills stick. When compared to a more formal test-driven and data valued classroom, it's easy to see how a relaxed vibe fosters more growth, confidence, and long-term retention. A relaxed classroom is an environment where curiosity can thrive, mistakes are welcomed, and students aren't afraid to take risks.

Darling-Hammond and Cook-Harvey share that "only 29% [of students] felt their school provided a caring, encouraging environment and fewer than half reported they had developed social competencies such as empathy, decision making, and conflict resolution skills."[1] Students are more willing to participate, ask questions, and explore ideas when they're not worried about being judged or getting everything right. In these settings, learning becomes a shared adventure rather than a stressful performance. Teachers who build relaxed atmospheres often see stronger relationships, deeper discussions, and more meaningful learning moments.

Joy is contagious, and when teachers show up relaxed, present, and having fun, students feel that energy. A calm and playful atmosphere invites everyone to be themselves, and that's when real learning happens. Don't just model content. Model the fun in learning. What if your classroom wasn't a stage where you have to perform, but a playground where you get to explore?

- Instead of obsessing over how it looks, ask yourself how it feels.
- Integrate play by adding a twist, a game, or a moment of silliness.
- Let students co-create parts of the day. Let them name activities, pick the music, or lead a movement break.

---

[1] Linda Darling-Hammond, Channa M. Cook-Harvey, and Learning Policy Institute. "Community Schools: An Evidence-Based Strategy for Equitable School Improvement." *LEARNING POLICY INSTITUTE RESEARCH BRIEF*, 2017. https://learningpolicyinsti tute.org/sites/default/files/product-files/Educating_Whole_Child_BRIEF.pdf.

Yes, teachers are bound by data and achievement in our classrooms, but our greatest impact goes well beyond data. Our greatest impact is creating a love of learning, and no one can measure that with numbers. Giving students a love of learning is life changing. I feel confident that every educator reading this book has countless stories about the impact they've made in a student's life. I too have those stories, but one child stands out.

I'll never forget the day Thomas walked into my second-grade classroom. His parents had already warned me: "He hates school." They explained that he didn't "dislike" or "struggle" with school; he hated school with a passion. Imagine a seven-year-old already hating school so much that his parents felt the need to "warn" the teacher. He missed his old school and had no interest in making this a smooth transition. When the first day rolled around, Thomas made his feelings known the second he crossed the doorway. He sat slouched in his chair with his arms crossed and a scowl on his face. He had thrown his backpack on the floor as if it had wronged him. "I hate school," he muttered under his breath, loud enough for everyone to hear. I greeted him with warmth and optimism, hoping a smile could melt some of that resistance, but it didn't. He barely looked at me.

Things only got bumpier from there. During a partner activity, he called another student a "dufus," and that was my line. I knelt beside him and gently, but firmly, let him know that I respected his feelings; however, I would not tolerate him calling another child names. I explained that all the kids deserve to come to school without having others call them names, and just like that, Thomas bolted right out of the classroom. Without missing a beat, I chased after him and caught up to him by the media center. He was panting and huffing. His little chest rising and falling with frustration and fear. When I walked up, I didn't scold, I crouched down and just breathed with him, and slowly, we made our way back to the classroom.

As we stepped back into the room, everyone looked at us. No one said a word. We just walked in, sat down, and I continued the first day of school as if nothing had happened. I called his dad that afternoon not as punishment, but as a continuation of the conversation his parents had started with me. "He's struggling," I told him, "but I'm not giving up on him," and I didn't.

Every day, Thomas came in with the same tough exterior, but I kept showing up with joy, consistency, and high expectations. I didn't lower the bar for him. Instead, I raised the fun around it. We played games with spelling words. We turned math into challenges. We laughed, a lot. Slowly, the scowl started to soften. He began to participate. He found little moments of success, and I made sure he saw them.

He was a gifted kid. That much was clear early on, but traditional learning just didn't spark anything in him. What did spark him? Imagination. Humor. Freedom. He didn't need more worksheets; he needed more wonder, and I adjusted. I met him halfway, and one day, without warning, he smiled as he walked into the room. That was the day I knew we were getting somewhere. By the end of the year, Thomas didn't just tolerate school, he loved it. He thrived in our classroom, not because I had all the answers, but because I gave him space to be himself and still belong. I saw Thomas as a child with flaws and fears but also with hope and wonder. I saw Thomas as a child with feelings. I looked beyond the data and test scores, and I simply saw Thomas.

Thomas is now a man, and I still talk to him and his parents from time to time, and they often tell me that I contributed to his success. Thomas's success wasn't just the result of one classroom or one teacher, it was a team effort. Alongside me were other educators who saw his potential and chose to nurture it, not contain it. Thomas' parents trusted the process, supported the boundaries we set, and celebrated the progress no matter how small. Together, we created a circle of support that gave Thomas what every child needs: consistency, compassion, belief, and fun. I played a part in his story, but so did many others. His growth was the result of a village that refused to give up on him, even when he made it difficult to hold on.

Of course, I teach the standards, and my lessons have learning objectives. I believe in academic rigor and giving students skills they need to succeed academically, but I also believe that learning should feel alive. So yes, we cover the content, but we might do it with a song, a silly voice, a scavenger hunt, or a paper airplane competition, because when students are having fun, they're engaged. Fun and high expectations are not opposites. I hold my students to high standards, and I also create a space where laughter is welcome, mistakes are celebrated, and every child feels safe to be themselves. Learning isn't less valuable because it's joyful; in fact, it's more meaningful when students connect with it emotionally. With that I challenge you, if you are not already doing so, to create a classroom space that evokes fun and warmth.

1. What's one moment from this week that made you smile? How can you build on it?
2. If you weren't worried about judgment, what would you try in your classroom?
3. What part of your authentic self have you been holding back? How can you let it shine this week?

Teaching isn't just about covering content; it's about seeing a student who walks in angry and recognizing that there's more to the story. It's about showing up, day after day, with patience, purpose, and joy even on the hard days. Thomas reminded me that sometimes the students who seem the hardest to reach are the ones who need us the most, and sometimes, all it takes is one adult who refuses to stop believing. You can be the teacher who blends rigor and spontaneity, and long after they've forgotten the spelling lists and math facts, they'll remember how it felt to be in your classroom.

CHAPTER 22

Too Much Pie: Establishing Boundaries

How do you balance loving your job and your students while also loving yourself?

Creating a space where our students can thrive is essential, but what about us? What about creating a space where teachers can thrive, too? For some reason, society cheers when corporate professionals prioritize themselves and their careers, but the moment a teacher talks about advancing their career, enjoying time off, or (*gasp*) taking a personal day, suddenly it's, "Don't you care about the kids?" I hear it all the time. "Why do you need a break? It must be nice to only work nine months a year." If you take one thing away from this book, make it this: Loving teaching doesn't mean losing yourself in the process. We can love our jobs, our students, *and* our weekends, take personal time, sick days, and countdown to holiday breaks.

According to a Gallup poll in 2022, "More than four in ten K-12 workers in the U.S. (44%) say they 'always' or 'very often' feel burned out at work, outpacing all other industries nationally." Researchers Marken and Agrawal go on to say, "The result is a workforce that is burned out and unfortunately leaving the profession at a high rate." They add, "For teachers nationally, a focus on alleviating that burnout has never been more important."[1] In other words? The alarm bells aren't just ringing, they're blaring. If we don't take burnout seriously, we risk losing the very people who make learning possible.

Let's talk about the elephant in the room: the teacher shortage. It's not just a headline or a hashtag. It's hitting schools across the U.S. in a big way. Districts are scrambling to fill classrooms, long-term subs are becoming the norm, and in some places, they're even pulling in retired educators or folks with provisional certifications just to keep the doors open, and it's not just math or science anymore, schools are struggling to find teachers in every subject, every grade level. It's a slow-burning crisis that's been building for years, and now it's impossible to ignore.

Why are teachers leaving? Is it burnout, low pay, unrealistic expectations, lack of support, being asked to do more with less, etc., or a combination of all? Maybe it's because teachers are expected to be educators, counselors, tech troubleshooters, behavior specialists, event planners, and sometimes even security guards, and for many, it just becomes too much. So, we simply leave. It's not because we don't care, but because we've cared for so long without being cared for in return.

Consider these research findings from D. Peck[2]:

- 86% of public school[s] struggle to hire educators.
- Less than 2 in 10 teachers are satisfied with their jobs.
- 51,000 teachers quit their jobs in the United States during 2023.
- 62% of teachers don't want their children to become teachers.
- 35% of teachers plan to quit in the next 2 years, down from 44%.
- There are more than 36,500 teacher vacancies in the United States.

---

[1] Marken, Stephanie, and Sangeeta Agrawal. "K-12 Workers Have Highest Burnout Rate in U.S." *Gallup.Com*, June 13, 2022. https://news.gallup.com/poll/393500/workers-highest-burnout-rate.aspx.

[2] "15 Teacher Shortage Statistics (2025) | Devlin Peck," n.d. https://www.devlinpeck.com/content/teacher-shortage-statistics.

There are so many factors causing teacher burnout, and time is at the top of that list. Much of the burnout comes from everything centered around teaching: endless meetings, lunch and recess duties, unpaid after-school commitments, new initiatives piled on top of old ones. Give teachers the time to focus on our craft, and we'll likely see the joy return. I am not suggesting that teachers only work contract hours; I am suggesting that teachers do what works best for them. If you're the type of teacher who enjoys arriving early to relish in the calm before the storm, or if you want to stay late or sponsor an after-school club, do what works best for you. If you do not take time for yourself, you may soon suffer from burnout.

When teachers ask me how to avoid teacher burnout, I like to have them visualize their teacher life on a paper plate. Imagine I hand you a paper plate and ask you to draw pie chart representing everything related to your teaching life (grading papers, graduate school, communicating with families, analyzing data, decorating your classroom, meetings, duties, IEPs, and even reading this book). You start dividing it into sections:

- 10% grading
- 10% decorating your classroom
- 50% teaching
- 10% parent communication
- 15% meetings
- 20% creating lesson plans
- 10% professional development
- 10% duties
- 5% mediating conflicts
- 5% tech troubleshooting

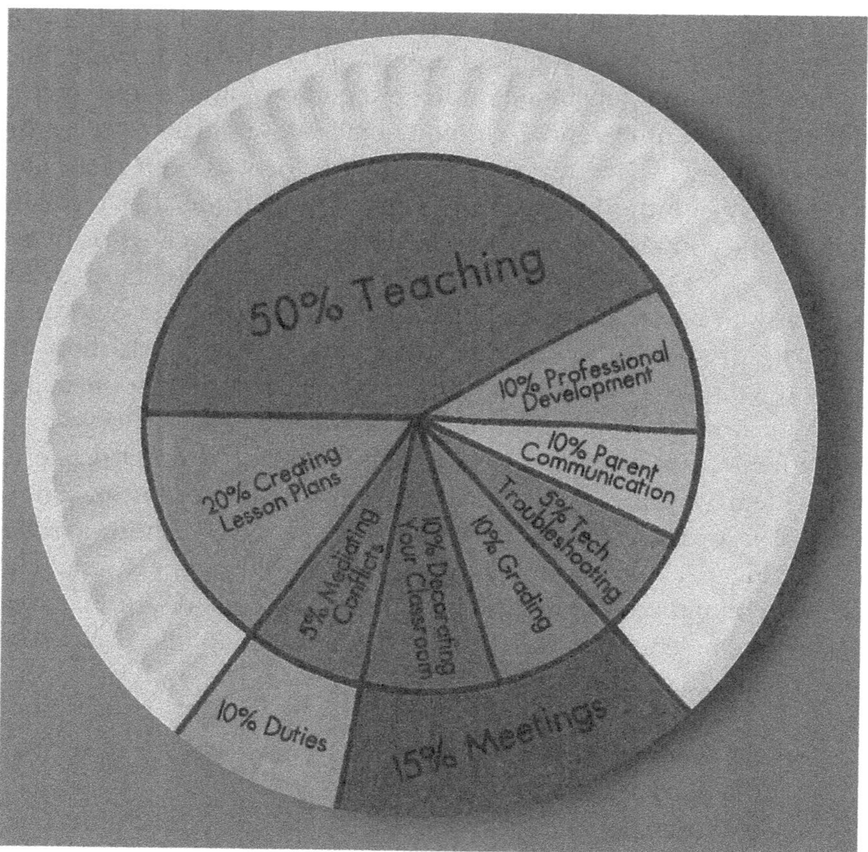

Wait a second. We're already at 145%, and we haven't even touched on extracurriculars, student behavior management, data analysis, and covering your classroom walls for state testing.

Somewhere along the way, teaching became a job that demands more than what's mathematically possible, and yet, most teachers keep going, giving 120%, 150%, even 200%. Teachers are told to "find your why and do it for the kids" thus creating more teacher guilt and burnout.

When we constantly operate beyond capacity, one of two things is happening. Either we're not doing everything as well as we think we are, or we're doing it all at a cost we can't sustain. Running on adrenaline, coffee, and willpower might hold things together for a while, but the cracks eventually show. Skipped lunches, late nights, and canceled appointments shouldn't be badges of honor. They're warning signs, not proof of dedication.

Next time you're scrolling through social media, search #teacherburnout. What you'll find isn't just a few isolated posts; it's a movement of teachers saying enough is enough. You'll see stories of educators leaving the profession, not because they stopped caring, but because they couldn't keep caring *at the expense of themselves.* They're bartending. They're working at Costco. They're opening Etsy shops or becoming real estate agents, and they're finding something in those jobs that teaching had taken from them: work-life-balance.

It doesn't have to come to that, but to stay in the profession and stay well, we must stop pretending we're invincible. We need to take charge by drawing our own lines, creating our own realistic pie charts, and guarding our 100%. This chapter isn't about guilt. It's about finding permission to say:

- I can't do everything.
- This task doesn't fit in with my 100% right now.
- My mental health matters just as much as my students' success.
- This weekend, I'm not grading. I'm recharging.
- No, I can't participate in the Sunshine or Field Day Committee.

Now take out a real paper plate and draw that pie chart. Force yourself to cap it at 100%. What do you want to prioritize? What can you let go of without getting fired? It's okay if something gets less attention this week. It doesn't make you a bad teacher. It makes you smart, strategic, and sustainable. So, the next time someone tries to hand you another slice of pie ask yourself, "Is there room on my plate," and if there's not, it's okay to say, "Nope, not right now."

Throughout the years I have discovered that if I do not protect my peace and energy, I will not be able to give my best to my students. To do that sometimes I simply need to say no. Remember the chess club I referred to in part one? The club that I had hoped would earn me a four on a four-point scale? When I realized that I was burning myself out and trying to sprint in a marathon, I came to the realization that it was no longer in my best interest to sponsor the Chess Club.

When I started teaching gifted education, I knew my days would be full of puzzles, projects, and moments of brilliance from the sharpest and most creative young minds. What I didn't expect was to accidentally launch one of the most popular chess clubs in all of Atlanta. I had taught my gifted education students how to play chess, and I thought, "Maybe I can lead a chess club after school to give other kids some exposure to chess." I created an online interest form and asked my principal to share it in The Principal's Newsletter. I would have one club for grades K-2 and another for grades 3–5. I figured a handful of kids might be interested. I imagined a quiet group of children eager to dive into the world of chess. What I got was something entirely different. Within months, the chess clubs exploded. Kids couldn't get enough. I was holding practice two days after school each week. We were attending tournaments on nights and weekends. Students who had never played chess were thriving in the chess club. I had created a little chess community at my school. We built friendships, confidence, strategic thinking, and the kind of joy that only comes from discovering a talent you didn't know you had. I was super busy with lessons, planning, parent emails, and chess tournaments. The chess club began to consume my planning period, weekends, and evenings, but it was worth it. The kids loved it. I loved it, and for three years, I gave it everything I had.

The following year came an announcement that would push my plate well past full. Administration informed me that I would now be assigned mandatory lunch and recess duties. When I pushed back and explained that I simply didn't have the time to take on even more, I was reassured that it wasn't a punishment. "We need teacher support to maintain the safety of the school and children," they said. I did the math. I was now required to spend 7.5 hours per week at these newly assigned duties. That's an entire workday, gone, and that's how burnout builds. It's not through one big event, but in small ways that eat away at your time, your energy, and your joy.

So, I made a decision. I quit the chess club. I did not quit out of spite or bitterness. I quit out of necessity for my mental health and well-being.

I was so focused on my administration and myself that I had not factored in the kids or parents of the chess club. One afternoon when I was standing at my newly minted dismissal duty post at the front of the school, a parent approached me along with his first-grade son. Apparently this wide-eyed first grader was looking forward to his turn in Ms. Chang's famous chess club. The parent looked at me, then down at his son, then back at me again and asked, "What happened to the chess club?" I told him I was no longer leading the club and referred him to various chess clubs nearby, and right there, in front of his child, he laid on the guilt. "You're going to abandon the kids just like that?" He wasn't mean about it, but he was clearly disappointed. You could tell he really cared, and yeah, that made the guilt sink in a little deeper than I expected.

I knelt and looked at his son and said, "I'm so sorry." Then I stood up, looked his father square in the eye, and said, "Yes, I understand that many chess kids will be disappointed, but my students and my own children will be delighted to have a better version of me. Therefore, I'm choosing my students, my family, and myself," and that was that. I walked away from the chess club.

When I can show up to class and give my students my best, they thrive, and yes, I too appreciated having my time back. Time to go on a walk, time to spend with my family, or time to simply recharge in the bathtub. I showed up fully for my students during the day. I showed up fully for my family at night and during the weekends and breaks. I took back my planning period to plan lessons and create resources. I didn't fade into the background as the teacher who "used to do cool stuff." I continued to thrive as the World's Okay-est teacher.

We live in a culture that worships the hustle. That praises "above and beyond." That glamorizes burnout as a badge of honor, but:

You don't have to do it all to be enough.

You don't have to be everything to everyone.

You can say no to good things in order to say yes to the best things.

I said yes to my family.

I said yes to my health.

I said yes to the version of me who doesn't have to prove her worth.

Guess what? The world kept spinning. The school kept running, and the chess kids kept learning and growing. So, if you're sitting with your own version of the chess club, but you're drowning under the weight of everything else, remember this:

Sometimes, the most courageous move isn't taking on more; it's stepping back.

It's saying no.

It's choosing to be okay, and being proud of that.

Checkmate.

CHAPTER 23

Learn from the Experts Down the Hall

Who in your school makes you a better teacher, and if given the opportunity, how would you thank them?

There's a lesson they don't teach you at conferences, in college, or during student teaching. It's not part of any professional development plan or listed in your teacher prep syllabus, but it's one of the most important truths I've learned time and time again. Sometimes, the most powerful thing a teacher can do is to take notes from someone who's quietly and consistently doing the work and doing it better than you.

These aren't always the loudest voices in the room. They may not be the ones leading the committee or presenting at staff meetings, but if you're paying attention, you'll find them. They're the ones who seem to anticipate problems before they arise, who interact with students and families with calm confidence, and who show up with the kind of wisdom that only comes from years of trial, error, and reflection. Learning from them makes you smarter, stronger, and more grounded in the reality that good teaching isn't a solo pursuit; it's a shared craft, and the best among us never stop being students.

In every school, there's an unsung hero, a quiet expert, the person who somehow knows exactly what to say to a parent, how to write an IEP with clarity and care, understands the laws in education, and can find the right form in the district database in seconds. For me, that person is Sherique Ransby. She's my gifted education teammate, and my guiding light. Ms. Ransby is more than a mentor. She's the colleague who truly understands and can help navigate even the worst of storms.

She doesn't wear a crown or seek the spotlight. In fact, you'll usually find her tucked away at her desk in a modest office connected to the back of her classroom. She's likely crafting a thoughtful response to yet another parent email, gently and professionally explaining the intricacies of gifted eligibility or calming anxieties about a recent assessment. While the rest of us are juggling a dozen visible tasks, she's handling a dozen invisible ones, each one critical, and each one handled with care, precision, and an unshakable calm.

While I'm busy designing fun and creative lesson plans and activities like kicking off the day with a joke to keep our gifted students smiling and curious, Ms. Ransby is managing the intricate web that makes our program work. She handles the behind-the-scenes magic such as assessments, paperwork, data, and deadlines. She's the one decoding testing reports and making sure everything we do is aligned with policy and best practice. She's five steps ahead, organized, deliberate, and deeply knowledgeable. She understands every facet of gifted education: the legal frameworks, the identification protocols, the service models, the complexities of twice-exceptionality, and the delicate balance between advocacy and accountability. If there's a question, she knows the answer. If there's a problem, she already has a solution, but what's most remarkable is that she doesn't flaunt it. She doesn't seek credit. She just does the work with quiet excellence and unwavering integrity.

Ms. Ransby is the kind of expert every educator deserves in their corner. She's the one who steps in not just when you ask for help, but often before you even realize you need it. Her presence alone brings a sense of reassurance, not because she has all the answers, but because she leads with grace, humility, and a deep belief in the work we do. I've learned so much simply by watching her, and I know without a doubt that I'm a better teacher and a better advocate for my students, because Ms. Ransby is part of my team.

If you're wondering what that kind of support looks like in real time, let me tell you about the morning everything could've gone off the rails. The first email arrived before I had even finished my morning coffee. The subject line read *Gifted Qualification Concern*, but the tone inside was far less polite. A father was upset that his first-grade daughter had not qualified for gifted education services, and he wanted answers. His message was long, bolded in places, and filled with rhetorical questions like, "How is this even possible?" and "Are you sure you understand how the process works?" As a professor at a local university, he seemed to imply that his academic title made him far more knowledgeable than me as just a simple elementary teacher. It was mansplaining on a whole new level.

When I receive emails that trigger an emotional response, I wait a few hours before responding to ensure that I respond professionally and without emotion. I outlined his daughter's scores and thoroughly explained that his daughter was not eligible for gifted education services at this time. Like always, I reassured him that his daughter was a bright and wonderful student, and we would continue to monitor and reevaluate her as needed. About ten minutes later he replied and copied my principal, but this time he was downright angry. The process was flawed, the results were inaccurate, and it was deeply concerning that someone like me was making these decisions.

I forwarded the email thread to Ms. Ransby, with a note that probably read something like, "Another Angry Parent Please Help," and just like that Ms. Ransby, "The Queen of Gifted" took control of the situation, and within minutes, she sent me a reply and asked if there was anything I wanted to add. Her message was calm, professional, and so thorough it could have been used as a training document for new gifted teachers. She included the exact Georgia DOE regulations, eligibility criteria by grade level, examples of testing instruments, and even broke down how motivation is calculated. She did all of this without a hint of annoyance. There were no CAPS, no exclamation points, just pure, polished expertise, and as expected the father never replied. No thank you, no further questions, not even a grudging acknowledgment. Just silence. For me that silence said everything.

When people ask how I survive in this role, I tell them the truth. I survive because I sit down the hall from a woman who knows everything and never flinches under pressure. She doesn't need a crown, but she deserves one. Early in our time working together, I had a choice to make. I could pretend I had it all figured out and act like I was just as experienced and knowledgeable as Ms. Ransby, or I could lean in. I could watch, listen, ask questions, and admit that I had and still have a lot to learn. I chose the latter path, and I am better for it. Without Ms. Ransby's guidance, I'm not sure I would've made it through that first year of gifted education intact. She answered my panicked texts, gently corrected me when I misunderstood policies, and reminded me more than once to breathe.

As teachers, it can be tempting to isolate ourselves, to feel like we have to always be the expert in the room, but there is something deeply freeing in acknowledging that we don't know everything, and that someone else might just be doing it better and that's okay. Growth starts with humility, and learning to admire, rather than compete, builds a culture of collaboration, not comparison, so look around your building and find the experts who are doing it better. Who's doing the excellent work? Who's a few steps ahead of you in experience or wisdom? Sit beside them and ask questions. Watch how they move. Say thank you, and don't be afraid to say, "I want to learn from you." We're not meant to do this alone. We grow stronger by learning from each other, especially from those who have already walked the path and are kind enough to lift you up and celebrate your success.

CHAPTER 24

Mindset Over Validation

What would you say to a student who's having a rough day, and do you extend the same advice to yourself?

Mentors can point you in the right direction, but your mindset is the engine that gets you there. In the last chapter, we talked about finding a mentor who believes in you and helps you see what's possible, but belief from others can only take you so far if you don't believe in yourself. The way you show up, the stories you tell yourself about your students, your school, and your ability all shape your experience far more than any curriculum map or checklist. If mentorship helps you see the path, your mindset decides whether you walk it with confidence or hesitation.

I wish someone would have told me early in my career that mindset is the most powerful classroom management tool you will ever have. It's not in your drawer next to the dry-erase markers. It's not on the district pacing guide, and it's not hiding in the rubric your evaluator uses to check boxes to rate your success. Your mindset is yours. You bring it with you every day, whether you realize it or not. Mindset either lifts you up or weighs you down, and sometimes, it does both. This chapter is not about pretending everything is fine when it clearly isn't. If your copy machine jammed, your observation got rescheduled during your most chaotic class, or a student just "accidentally" threw their yogurt at the ceiling, then yeah, it's okay to say it was a rough day, but what we can't do is live in that place forever. There is a difference between acknowledging struggle and surrendering to it.

Many teachers, me included, seem to crave validation. It's not because teachers are needy. It's because teaching asks us to give endlessly. Most days, what we get back isn't pay or praise, it's the quiet satisfaction of knowing we showed up for the kids who need us the most. Teachers start chasing little signs that we're doing well. Whether it's a compliment from a parent, an excellent observation score, or a student who writes "you're my favorite teacher" in messy handwriting on a crumpled sticky note, these things matter. However, if we continue to wait for validation from others, we may never find happiness within ourselves.

I wish I could say I stopped seeking gold stars after elementary school, but that would be a lie. Somewhere deep down, I still want someone with a clipboard and a title to walk into my classroom, see the magic, and say, "Wow. You're doing something really special here." I don't want a parade or a plaque, but I crave validation from someone higher up telling me that I matter.

Early in my career, I bent over backward to make sure my room looked just right before walk-throughs. I'd tweak lesson plans to make them more "observable," add extra engagement strategies, even rehearse transitions in my head like I was preparing for opening night. If an administrator was stepping in, even for five minutes, I wanted it to be the best five minutes of their day, and sometimes, it worked. I got the nod. The quick "Nice job" on the way out, but often, it didn't land that way. I'd spend hours preparing only to hear nothing, or worse, I'd get a checklist with comments like, "Try to increase rigor" or "Consider more student voice." These comments often left me feeling disconnected from what had actually just happened in the room. Their silence was louder than any critique. It made me question my worth.

What I didn't realize then is that *I was outsourcing my sense of worth*. I was handing it to people who, through no fault of their own, were juggling a thousand other priorities. They didn't see the hours I spent calling families or the careful scaffolding I built into a lesson so a struggling reader could finally shine. I was expecting people to notice invisible labor, and when they didn't, I took it personally. I still do. Here's the hard truth that admittingly I too am still working on. *When you rely on external validation to fuel your internal fire, you'll burn out every single time.*

Finding Value in Self-Worth

The shift didn't happen all at once, but little by little, I started giving myself the credit I had been so desperate to hear from someone else. I started asking myself, "Did I show up with heart today? Did I make a kid feel seen? Did I lead with integrity even when it was hard?" If the answer was yes, I let that be enough, and on the days when I fell short, I gave myself grace, not because I didn't care, but because I cared so deeply. I learned to validate myself not out of arrogance, but out of necessity.

It's not that I don't still hope for kind words or recognition from leadership. Of course I do. We all want to feel seen, but I've stopped letting their silence shrink me. My work is not less valuable just because someone didn't clap. To any teacher reading this who feels unseen, please know your worth is not measured by walk-throughs or evaluation rubrics. The impact you have is real, even when it goes unacknowledged. You don't need a gold star to keep shining. I've never been Teacher of the Year. Not once. No shiny plaque, no balloon bouquet delivered to my room, no surprise announcement over the loudspeaker while the staff claps politely. I've clapped for others while wishing I too would receive more recognition, and to this day I continue to be a three-point teacher on a four-point evaluation scale, and yet, something happened recently that reminded me why I've never needed it.

I was mindlessly scrolling through TikTok on a random Sunday afternoon when I saw I had a new message. I wasn't expecting much. Usually it's just spam or someone asking where I got my classroom rug, but this one caught my eye. It was from a parent I hadn't heard from in years. Her son, a student I had taught many years ago, was graduating from college. She said she had come across one of my videos and just had to reach out. She told me he still talks about my class and that I was his all-time favorite teacher. I sat with her kind and genuine words and reflected. Honestly, I reread the message a few times letting it sink in that I made a lasting impact regardless of the lack of recognition I had received.

I remember this kid so well. He was wildly smart. As a matter of fact, he is only one of three kids to ever beat me at chess in my twenty-plus years of teaching. He had this incredible way of thinking that didn't always fit into the neat little boxes school tries to create.

Other kids didn't always get him. Some teachers didn't either, but I saw something in him. He was bright. He was kind. He was bursting with ideas and questions. I knew from early on that trying to force him to be "normal" would just flatten everything special about him. I celebrated him and gave him a space to simply be himself, and now here he was, years later, graduating from college. His mom wrote that he told her I was one of the first people who truly celebrated who he was. I didn't try to fix him or change him or quiet him. He said it was teachers like me who helped him believe that being brilliant was something good.

Her words remind me that the most meaningful recognition we ever get as teachers doesn't come from administrators or ceremonies. It comes in moments like this. When a kid who used to be underestimated remembers you as the person who saw his magic. When a family reaches out after all those years to say thank you. That's the real stuff. That's the kind of award that doesn't collect dust. So no, I've never been Teacher of the Year, and I will likely continue being scored as "average" on the state's rating scale, but I am his teacher for life. Honestly, that's enough for me. We have got to stop letting test scores and evaluations decide whether we're "good enough." We are not spreadsheets. We are not checklists. We are humans who shape other humans, and the truth is, the best parts of teaching are often immeasurable.

Your Legacy in Stories

Now let's go one step deeper. What happens if we stop tying our identity as educators to things we can't control such as low-test scores, a mediocre evaluation, or even a parent complaint. If we let those things define us, then we are constantly handing over our peace to someone else. That is not sustainable. That is not fair to us, and it's not fair to our students either, because when we are burnt out and bitter, they feel it. There is a difference between a tough day and a toxic environment. There is a difference between coworkers who are real and coworkers who are relentless. You know the type. The ones who act like hope is a character flaw or the ones who treat every new initiative like it's a personal attack. Spending too much time on that negative energy will change you.

It won't happen overnight, but it will begin to consume you. At first, you're just nodding along in the break room, but then you're joining in and adding your own complaints. Before you realize, you're expecting the worst before it even happens, and just like that, you've become part of the very culture that's draining you.

In her research, Kori L. Friedges', a psychology student at the College of Saint Benedict and Saint John's University, research reminds us:

> ...positives in the present moment can increase aspects of positive affect, and that focusing and reflecting on the negatives in the present moment can reduce your happiness. Simply, a negative mindset has the power to detract from happiness and heighten negative emotions. This is worth noting because if you choose to only think about the negatives, then you will feel negatively as well. But, if you choose to interpret and view the present situation with a positive mindset, you have the power to experience more positive affect.[1]

Changing your mindset is not about pretending everything is fine, and it's not about ignoring what is hard or acting like everything is perfect when it clearly is not. It is about protecting your peace. It is about choosing yourself even when things feel heavy. It means noticing the small wins. It means reminding yourself that progress does not always show up on a spreadsheet. It means giving yourself credit for what you do every single day that no one else sees, because some days will be exhausting. Some days you will question your impact. You will wonder if anything you are doing is enough. That is exactly when you need to pause and remember that your value was never in a test score or a rubric. Your impact is in the stories. It is in the kids who remember how you made them feel. It is in the quiet victories and the long-term growth you may never fully see, so, protect your mindset. Be thoughtful about where you

---

[1] Friedges, Kori L. *The Effect of a Positive and Negative Mindset on Affect, Happiness, and Heart Rate Variability*. CSBSJU Distinguished Thesis 1, College of Saint Benedict and Saint John's University, 2020. https://digitalcommons.csbsju.edu/ur_thesis/1.

spend your energy, and when in doubt, turn back to your students and the work you do with them. That is where the truth is. That is where the real reward lives.

If you're feeling worn out or stuck in a cycle of doubt, pause and think about your own version of this moment. Maybe it was a student who wrote you a thank-you note years later. Maybe it was a quiet kid who finally found their voice in your classroom. Maybe it was a parent who told you that their child never felt seen until you came along. Whatever it is, hold onto that. Let that be the thing that helps you shift your mindset when the job feels too big, or when the system feels too broken. You don't need a plaque to prove your worth. You just need to remember the impact you've already made because those stories are your legacy.

CHAPTER 25

What It Means to Lead Together

What would a school culture look like if teachers and administrators truly worked together?

Administrators, I have so much respect for you and anyone who chooses this path. Leading a school takes courage, vision, and an incredible amount of heart. As a teacher, I often wonder what inspired your decision to lead, guide, and to carry the weight of so many moving parts. This chapter is my way of exploring that relationship and how we can build stronger bridges between our worlds.

Seriously, what led you to the front office? Maybe you started out in the classroom and felt called to make a bigger impact beyond it, or maybe your path looked different. Perhaps you came through counseling, coaching, or another leadership route that put you right where you're needed most. Was it the dream of shaping a whole school's culture? The challenge of solving big-picture problems, or maybe, just maybe, it was the idea of finishing your coffee while it's still hot. (No judgment! Every teacher understands that dream.) Whatever your journey, I'm genuinely curious about what drew you here and what keeps you going.

No matter what your reason, I hope it was because you believed you could make a difference on a larger scale, because stepping into school leadership is no small leap. It takes guts, vision, and a whole lot of heart, because when you're doing the job well, it's way more than meetings and master schedules. You're nurturing a culture, protecting the joy of teaching, and helping entire communities grow stronger. You're in a position to build people up or wear them down, and that kind of influence is powerful. So, to every administrator out there leading with integrity and care, thank you. We see you. We need you.

We need you more than we sometimes admit, but not in a vague, distant way. We need you to be with us, not above us. We need your support, your consistency, your clarity, and your ability to shield us from some of the nonsense that tries to trickle down into our classrooms. We need you to stop asking us to "remember our why" every time we're drowning. We know our why. What we need is a how. We need a who. We need you. Schools need you. According to Louis, Leithwood, Wahlstrom, and Anderson, "leadership is second only to classroom instruction among all school-related factors that contribute to what students learn at school" and "while evidence about leadership effects on student learning can be confusing to interpret, much of the existing research actually underestimates its effects."[1] Throughout this book, I've shared strategies and ideas meant to help teachers not just survive but thrive, but none of it works without strong, supportive leadership. I've asked teachers what contributes most to burnout, and the number one answer, almost every time, is "a lack of administrative support." It's not low pay, difficult parents or even kids these days. It all ties back to leadership. When teachers feel supported, they thrive; they're more likely to stay, and that makes a difference in the school community. The best administrators don't just manage a school, they build trust. They ask for feedback and truly listen. They show up at recess and sit in on hard conversations with parents. They recognize who's overwhelmed before the meltdown happens, and they step in without being asked. They understand that data matters, but dignity matters more.

---

[1] Learning from Leadership Project, Investigating the Links to Improved Student Learning, Karen Seashore Louis, Kenneth Leithwood, Kyla L. Wahlstrom, and Stephen E. Anderson, 2010. https://wallacefoundation.org/sites/default/files/2023-10/Investigating-the-Links-to-Improved-Student-Learning.pdf.

That's what good leadership looks like. Good leaders don't have to fix everything. They simply need to show up, listen, and trust their staff. Administrators can offer support in so many ways, and while student behavior often takes center stage, there are many ways to support their teachers. For example:

- **Presence:** Be visible in classrooms and hallways not just for evaluation, but for encouragement and connection.
- **Listening:** Make space for teacher input before decisions are finalized.
- **Empowerment:** Trust teachers to try new ideas and know they'll be backed up, even if things don't go perfectly.
- **Transparency:** Communicate clear expectations, policies, and priorities so teachers feel informed.
- **Recognition:** Celebrate both big wins and small daily victories.
- **Balance:** Protect planning time, honor boundaries, and model self-care for the entire staff.

These aren't grand gestures. They're daily habits that remind teachers they're seen, valued, and part of a team that believes in them. When life throws something unexpected, teachers don't remember the latest school initiative or spreadsheet, they remember who reached out, who made space, and who cared.

It was a Monday morning like any other until it wasn't. I walked into school, holding my kindergarten son's hand ready to begin the day. Then my sister called. Her voice was shaking as she told me our mom had suffered a massive heart attack and was being rushed into emergency open-heart surgery. Everything around me seemed to slow down, then speed up all at once. My feet kept moving, but my heart felt like it had collapsed. I could feel the tears start to fall before I even made it through the front doors.

The world blurred as I walked inside, trying to process the unimaginable. That's when my principal saw me. She didn't hesitate. She didn't wait for an explanation. She walked straight toward me with eyes full of concern and calm. "Are you okay?" she asked gently. I tried to respond, but the words got stuck somewhere between panic and heart attack. She took one look at my son and said, "Hey buddy, let's get you settled." Then she asked the media specialist to walk him to class so he wouldn't see his mom fall apart, and then she turned to me. She held my shoulders and looked me right in the eyes. She did not speak as my boss. She was simply a human being who saw another human in pain. She said, "Go. Do whatever you need to do. School isn't going anywhere." There was no talk of leave requests or questions about sub plans. She was genuinely concerned and gave me the unconditional support I simply needed at that time. I wasn't just a teacher juggling lesson plans, I was a daughter trying to hold it all together, and once again, my administration didn't just talk about supporting staff, they lived it. My principal gave me the space, grace, and trust I needed to step away and be with my family and myself.

My mom spent the next two weeks in the critical care ICU, and every day was a relentless swing between hope and fear. I was driving four hours round trip, trying to be everything to everyone: daughter, mom, sister, wife, and still somehow, a teacher. I was running on adrenaline, late-night fast food, whispered prayers in hospital parking lots, and sheer willpower. Every beep of her monitor sent my heart racing, each doctor's update hanging in the air like a verdict. I didn't know what each hour would hold. Some days, we saw small signs of progress. Other days, we held our breath and braced for the worst, and in the middle of all that chaos and uncertainty, do you know what I didn't feel? Pressure. Guilt. The creeping anxiety so many educators know all too well. The worry that taking time to care for your family will somehow count against you. That wasn't my reality. I checked in when I could. I responded to a few emails, a text or two, and I would teach a few hours before driving back to the hospital.

No one from my school leadership made me feel like I wasn't doing enough. There were no passive-aggressive reminders, no guilt-tripping about sub plans or coverage. My principal never once asked when I was coming back. Instead, she asked how my mom was doing. She asked how I was doing. My school community showed up for me in quiet and steady ways that said, "Take care of what matters. We've got you," and that mattered. It mattered more than words can express. When people talk about what makes a great leader, they often list off strategies, data, and goals, but in that moment, it wasn't a policy or a protocol that made the difference, it was humanity. I will never forget it.

Sadly, a miracle never came. After a brave fight, my mom lost her battle as sepsis took over her body. In her final moments, my three siblings and I were by her side as she took her last breath. We held her hands, whispered our love, and said goodbye in the most sacred and heartbreaking way imaginable, and even in that grief, I found myself grateful that I had been given the time and support to show up fully for her.

As a retired teacher, my mother knew the pressures educators face, the unrelenting demands, the emotional weight we carry. I know without a doubt she would have been thankful that I had a school family who didn't just say they cared, they showed it. They allowed me to step away from the role of teacher so I could show up fully as a daughter, and that is a gift I will never forget.

Some administrators are doing this beautifully, and I see you. We all see you. We talk about you in hushed tones of appreciation. You're the reason some of us are still here. You're the one who pulled us aside when we looked like we were barely hanging on. You're the one who said, "Take a personal day, I've got your back." You're the one who treats us like professionals, not liabilities. Thank you for that, but there are other leaders who mean well but miss the mark. Some deliver inspirational slogans in meetings but disappear when a parent calls to scream at us. Some of you remind us to be data-driven but never ask how we're doing as people. Some leaders say they have an open-door policy but appear irritated when we walk through the door. To those leaders, we need more from you. We need fewer posters in the lounge and more action. We need follow-through. We need fairness. We need to be seen. Sometimes we simply need you to say, "Hi how are you doing? Do you need anything from me?" We need you to mean it and trust us to know what our students need. Trust us to try something different without fear of being penalized. Trust us to have hard conversations with you, not because we're complaining, but because we care deeply. If you create a culture where trust is the foundation, everything else becomes possible. Innovation becomes possible. Joy becomes possible. Longevity becomes possible, and teachers stay, thrive, and the culture of the school flourishes.

I know the pressure on you is intense. I know you're dealing with district mandates, parent complaints, budgets, board meetings, and so much more. I do not envy your position, but the best administrators are the ones who take all that stress and somehow still lead with heart. You don't have to fix everything, but we need to know you're in the work with us. At the end of the day, teachers do not expect perfection. We don't need you to have all the answers. What we do need is to know you see us and that you believe in us. We want you to respect the incredible weight we carry each day, and when things get hard, you'll be standing beside us and not watching from a distance with a checklist.

Here's to the school leaders who support and lead with empathy, and who haven't forgotten what it's like to stand in front of a class with a glitching interactive whiteboard and a lesson that may or may not make sense. Here's to the school leaders who understand that sometimes only one kid is listening while five others are wiggling around or counting the ceiling tiles. We need you, and we are so much better when we have you in our corner.

Conclusion

What's that one story that made you realize that you became the teacher you needed?

If you've made it this far in the book, then you already understand that teaching is more than just a job. It's demanding, unpredictable, and often overwhelming. Some days you walk out of your classroom feeling proud and certain that you're doing exactly what you're meant to be doing. Other days, you find yourself scrolling through job listings and wondering what it would be like to work somewhere quiet, with headphones on, and no one asking for a pencil. Some days the work feels like chaos, but it's also meaningful and you can see the difference you're making. There is a sense of fulfillment that is hard to find anywhere else. As I look back on my own journey, I realize I didn't just become a teacher. I became the teacher I always needed. Every chapter of this book tells part of the story of how I became the teacher I once needed, the one who led with heart, laughter, and humanity. The lessons weren't learned all at once; they came in small, humbling moments, student by student, year by year.

Chapter 10: More Than Showing Up: How Trust Turns Classrooms into Communities

I became the teacher I needed when I learned that showing up isn't just about attendance, it's about presence. Trust doesn't come from titles; it grows from consistency. When students see that you mean what you say, that you listen without judgment, and that you'll show up tomorrow even after a hard day, that's when a classroom becomes a community.

Chapter 11: More Than a Smile: The Power of Joyful Classrooms

I learned that joy isn't just an added bonus, it's a bridge that connects teachers and students. A joyful classroom isn't one where everything is perfect; it's one where laughter and learning happen side by side. I became the teacher I needed when I let fun and curiosity lead the way, even on the hard days.

Chapter 12: Oops, Now What? When Humor Goes Too Far

I learned that humor has power, but it also has responsibility. The teacher I needed would have known how to say "I'm sorry" when a joke missed the mark. Apologizing to a student doesn't diminish authority; it builds trust. That's what I learned from Michael, because the power of humility helps us grow and become better versions of ourselves.

Chapter 13: The Courage to Ask for Help

I became the teacher I needed when I stopped pretending I could do it all alone. Asking for help isn't a sign of weakness; it's an act of courage. Support from colleagues, administrators, or even students reminds us that teaching is a team sport, and we're stronger together.

Chapter 14: Recharge, Rethink, Reignite: Smarter PD for the Tired Teacher

I used to think professional development meant sitting through slides and strategies that I already knew. Then I realized that growth happens when teachers see themselves as students who never stop learning. The teacher I needed valued PD as an opportunity to grow, reflect, recharge, and reconnect us to our purpose.

Chapter 15: Becoming Better Without Burning Out

I became the teacher I needed when I learned that improvement doesn't require self-sacrifice. Growth can coexist with rest. You don't have to run on empty to make a difference. Balance doesn't make you less committed; it makes you sustainable.

Chapter 16: Finding Value in Creative Thinking

I learned that creativity is the heart of problem-solving. The teacher I needed gave students permission to think differently and make mistakes. Creativity keeps curiosity alive for both students and teachers.

Chapter 17: The Genius of Amplifying Student Voices

I became the teacher I needed when I learned to stop being the loudest voice in the room. Real teaching is listening. Empowering students to share ideas, lead projects, and speak their truths transforms classrooms into communities of thinkers.

Chapter 18: Finding Mentors in Unlikely Places

The teacher I needed believes that mentorship can come from anywhere: a colleague, a student, or even a mistake. Every person who challenges or supports us adds to our growth. I learned to stay open to wisdom in all its forms.

Chapter 19: Create the Career You Desire

I became the teacher I needed when I stopped waiting for permission to evolve. Teaching can look many different ways. You can stay in the classroom and still expand your impact, or step into new roles while keeping your roots in education.

Chapter 20: Protecting Your Peace One Parent at a Time

I learned that protecting your peace isn't selfish; it's essential. The teacher I needed could partner with parents while holding healthy boundaries. Relationships with families are strongest when built on respect, clarity, and care.

Chapter 21: Have Fun and Teach Like Nobody's Watching

I became the teacher I needed when I let go of perfection. The best lessons are rarely the prettiest ones. Some of the best moments happen when the plan goes sideways but the learning still shines through.

Chapter 22: Too Much Pie: Establishing Boundaries

I learned that saying yes to everything doesn't make you a better teacher; it just makes you a tired one. The teacher I needed knew when to say no, when to rest, and when to step back so they could show up better tomorrow.

Chapter 23: Learn from the Experts Down the Hall

I became the teacher I needed when I stopped comparing myself to others and started collaborating. There's brilliance in every hallway if you're humble enough to seek it. The teacher I needed wasn't afraid to learn from others or to admit she didn't know it all.

Chapter 24: Mindset Over Validation

I learned that the validation I craved as a young teacher (awards, praise, perfect scores) wasn't the point. The teacher I needed found peace in knowing her worth even without applause. True validation comes from the faces of students who feel seen and not from plaques on a wall.

Chapter 25: What It Means to Lead Together

I became the teacher I needed when I realized leadership isn't about position, it's about partnership. The best schools thrive when teachers and administrators work together. We don't build culture from the top down; we build it side by side.

Every chapter, every mistake, every student has been part of becoming the teacher I needed as a child. If you're reading this, I hope you see that you're already becoming the teacher you always needed.

Keep showing up. Keep learning. Keep leading with heart. The work you do doesn't just teach, it heals.

In the beginning, I'll admit it, I wanted the recognition and sometimes I still do. I hoped for the awards, the perfect evaluations, the emails from administrators that said, "You're doing an exceptional job." I wanted some kind of official validation that I was getting it right, but the truth is, I rarely get perfect scores. As a matter of fact, most of my observations came with the same kind of feedback that so many teachers hear. I need more anchor charts. I need to make sure my standards are clearly posted. I needed to increase the level of rigor in my lessons. I needed to write more data-driven goals that aligned with the school's initiatives. It's not that I'm not trying or that my lessons aren't effective. In fact, I pour everything I have into my students every day, but somehow, when it comes time to evaluate my performance, the focus always seems to find the miss rather than the things I am doing well.

I catch myself thinking these things, and then I remember the moment earlier that week when a student hugged me goodbye and whispered, "You are the reason I like coming to school." I think of the parent who emailed to say thank you for noticing their child's anxiety before it became a bigger problem. I think of the quiet student who finally raised their hand in April after months of staying silent. These are not the kinds of moments that win you plaques. They're not flashy or easy to showcase, but they are real. They are meaningful, and they are why I stay.

I never became a surgeon like I once dreamed of when I was a kid. However, somewhere along the way, I stepped into a role that is just as impactful and heals in its own lasting way. I became a teacher. Teaching may not involve scalpels or giving a child like me the ability to walk, but the work we do in classrooms changes and saves lives every day. I found a kind of healing that doesn't happen in an operating room but in small everyday moments like when a kid who usually keeps their head down finally starts to speak up, or when you help a student realize they're capable and that they matter. Surgeons save lives and so do teachers.

Helping kids believe in themselves and in their future doesn't require a medical degree, but it can be just as powerful. It's a different kind of healing, and I wouldn't trade it for anything.

I think about Michael often, and if you've been reading along, you know about him. He was the bright, spirited, challenging first grader who got under my skin and into my heart in equal measure. He pushed my buttons and one day, in a moment I'm not proud of, I called him a "butt." I apologized, admitted I was wrong, and explained how I would do better not just for Michael, but all my future students. Years passed and he moved away in ninth grade. I assumed he had long forgotten me until the summer before he left for college. Michael's mom emailed me and invited me to brunch. Michael, now a young man heading to college, wanted to see me. Over that meal, he looked me in the eye and said, "Of all my teachers, you made the greatest impact, Ms. Chang." It wasn't about a perfect lesson plan, anchor charts, rigor, or test scores. What stayed with Michael had nothing to do with data points or evaluation rubrics. It was the way I saw him and as Michael said, "You simply treated me like a person." I let him be himself even on the most challenging days. Of course, I taught the standards and pushed him academically, but what mattered most was the relationship and space I created where he felt safe, capable, and respected. That was the real impact, and that is exactly what made the difference in his life. That moment will stay with me forever. It reminded me that our greatest power as teachers don't come from our content knowledge or our management systems. It comes from our humanity and our commitment to change lives.

Then there's Ellie. I ran into her dad at a gas station one Sunday afternoon. I was rushing to get home when he approached me and thanked me for helping Ellie deal with Mondays. Ellie hated Sunday nights because she didn't want to go to school the following morning. However, she had recently begun to love Mondays, because it was her gifted education day with Ms. Chang. He explained that on Mondays, Ellie would leap out of bed cheering, "It's Monday! It's Ms. Chang day!" That's the power of being seen. That's the difference one teacher, one class, one connection can make. We don't always get to see the ripple effect of what we do, but when we do, it's everything.

There are so many other stories. So many kids who have made me laugh until I cried, or cry until I laughed. The ones who brought me birthday cards made of construction paper and glitter. There were the ones who wrote "I love you Ms. Chang" in the corner of their math test. Some kids drove me absolutely bananas, then hugged me on the last day of school like I had saved their world.

There was Kira who refused to speak for weeks, then slowly began answering yes-or-no questions with a nod before eventually sharing her chicken stories with the class. Kira barely spoke during the first few months of third grade. She was one of those students who sat quietly, did everything she was supposed to do, and avoided attention. If I called on her, her voice came out as a whisper. If other kids laughed or played loudly, she often shrunk into her seat just a little more. She wasn't unhappy. She was just deeply shy. She's the kind of kid who flies under the radar if you're not paying close enough attention.

One afternoon during our class optional share time Kira raised her hand. I tried to act casual, but I was elated, and when I asked her to share, she quietly said, "I have chickens." It was the softest sentence, but to me, it felt like Kira was shouting to the world. I didn't waste a second. I lit up, but I played it casual. "Kira! You have chickens? Tell us everything!" Kira blinked, surprised by my excitement, and nodded. I asked what kind of chickens. How many, and if they had names. She shook her head no, implying that her chickens did not have names to which I joked, "You should name one Ms. Chang." That made her literally laugh out loud. It was the kind of laugh you remember because it means something cracked open, yes chicken egg pun intended, in the best possible way.

Two days later, I received an email from Kira's mom, and attached was a photo of a fluffy black and white hen staring into the trail camera from the backyard. The subject line? *Meet Ms. Chang the Chicken.* I showed the class the chicken photo the following week, and they were obsessed. Kira beamed while her classmates asked questions about her chicken's alter ego. Suddenly, the quietest girl in class had become the keeper of a classroom legend. Each week after that, Kira would give us an update during our morning meeting. Kira began to share full-on chicken tales. One week, Ms. Chang the chicken had jumped on the trampoline, and another week, she landed squarely on Kira's head. A few weeks later, Ms. Chang the chicken allegedly pecked her way through a cardboard box maze built by Kira and her sister. We never quite knew what to expect, but we always knew it would be good. Kira wasn't just talking; she was a storyteller.

Kira's transformation didn't happen because I taught a flawless lesson or followed a script. It happened because I listened, and I got excited about something that mattered to her. Sometimes the best teaching isn't about standards or structure. It's about chickens. It's about creating space where a kid like Kira feels brave enough to speak, and when she does, we cheer. We celebrate. We name a chicken after ourselves and watch what happens next. Ms. Chang the chicken may never win a blue ribbon, but she helped a shy third grader find her voice in school.

There are so many students and stories to count, and I am sure there are many who never said thank you directly but showed it in the way when they sat a little taller, smiled a little wider, or tried just a little harder in a space where they felt safe. Teaching is about belonging. It is about creating a classroom where kids feel like they matter and can see a future they want to walk into. Yes, the work is hard. Yes, there are days when you question everything, but there are also days when you realize you were the turning point for someone. You were the moment that changed their mind about school or even themselves.

Sometimes I wish I could call my mom and tell her all of this. I want to share these wins. I want to hear her say, "I'm proud of you." I want to share Michael's words with her, tell her about Ellie, or Ms. Chang the Chicken. I want to know that I made my mom proud, but even though I can't call her, I carry her with me in so many ways. My mother taught me to focus on myself and to not let others design my journey, and to you, if you are a teacher reading this, please remember, you are someone's Michael story. You are the reason someone smiled on a Monday. You are the teacher they will talk about when they are grown. They may not say it now. You may never hear it at all, but your presence matters. Your work matters. You matter. Keep showing up. Keep leading with heart and know that even if the world doesn't always see it, you are changing the world one child at a time.

Acknowledgments

For my mom, who is no longer here but forever changed the course of my life when she let me advocate for myself in high school. That single act taught me that my voice mattered, and it continues to shape the way I teach, parent, and live today.

For my best friend, Betsy, who has walked with me, literally and figuratively, through every page of this book. From Saturday morning walks to long coffee shop conversations, thank you for listening to every story, laughing at every memory, and reminding me that my words were worth sharing.

For my educator colleagues who continue to support me. Your support through every high and low has meant more than words can express. Thank you for celebrating my wins and standing beside me when the road was hard, but especially my gifted teammate, Sherique Ransby. Without you, there is no way I would continue to thrive in the world of gifted education.

Mrs. Edwards, thank you for seeing something in me before I could see it in myself. You didn't just teach English literature and grammar. You taught me to believe in myself, and that belief would carry me through college and into a future where I too have the opportunity to impact my students in the same way.

To everyone at Wiley Jossey-Bass, thank you for believing in this book from the start.

To Ashante, my acquisition editor, for convincing me that my story and wisdom were worth sharing, and to Sunnye and Debbie, my editors, who truly earned their paychecks and helped shape my words into something far greater than I could have imagined.

To everyone who has followed, laughed, learned, and lifted me up along the way, thank you. Your support turned a simple hobby into a community, a career, and now a book. This exists because you showed up for me.

For my children, Jackson (12) and Fox (10), who make my life complete. You are my greatest joy, my best teachers, and my daily reminder of why the work of love, inclusion, and creativity matters.

And most of all, for my wife, Tsui Mei, who believed in me when I did not believe in myself. You encourage me to take risks, but also to say no when the weight is too much. You celebrate every success, no matter how great or small, and you cheer for me when I feel invisible. This book is possible because of your steady love, your endless support, and the way you make me feel seen, always.

Author's Bio

Jere Chang has spent over 20 years teaching in K-12 schools, with the last decade dedicated to gifted education. Known for her ability to celebrate every student's unique strengths, Chang believes that all children deserve to feel valued, included, and inspired.

With over four million followers on social media, "Ms. Chang" has become a trusted voice for educators, parents, and students who want to see creativity, curiosity, and joy at the heart of learning. She shares classroom moments, family adventures, and even her teaching "oops" with honesty and humor reminding others that teaching is as much about connection as it is about content.

A Distinguished University of Georgia Alumna, Chang holds three master's degrees in TESOL, college administration, and applied linguistics. She has spent her career helping students think critically, explore creatively, and see themselves as capable of big ideas. Her writing and content shine a light on the power of inclusion, the importance of equity, and the beauty of seeing the world through a child's perspective.

She lives in Atlanta, Georgia with her wife and their two children. Together, they enjoy taking walks through their neighborhood, traveling to new places, and spending time at the lake where they can slow down, connect, and make memories as a family.